GW00683541

Sanctuary

A collection of essays based upon talks given by the Temenos Academy
at The Prince's Foundation during the academic year 2002–2003,
with a Foreword by His Royal Highness The Prince of Wales

Sanctuary

Edited by DAVID CADMAN and JOHN CAREY

TEMENOS ACADEMY

TEMENOS ACADEMY PAPERS NO. 23

First published 2006 by
The Temenos Academy
16 Lincoln's Inn Fields
London WC2A 3ED

Registered Charity no. 1043015

Copyright © The Contributors

ISBN 0 9540311 7 2 *cased*
ISBN 0 9540311 8 0 *paper*

*All rights reserved. No part of this book
may be reproduced in any way without
the prior permission of the publisher.*

Typeset by Agnesi Text, Hadleigh
Printed in the United Kingdom
at Smith Settle, Yeadon

Frontispiece:
Stones of the West Wall of the
Temple in Jerusalem

Foreword

HRH The Prince of Wales

As Patron of the Temenos Academy, it has always been my hope that this Academy would work together with my Foundation for the Built Environment to celebrate and honour that which we might call 'The Sacred Tradition'. I was therefore delighted when, during the academic year 2002–3, they came together to arrange a series of lectures to explore the theme of 'sanctuary' within the great spiritual traditions, and I am pleased to see that this has now led to this rather beautiful book.

With the exception of Alastair Duncan's video on 'The Noble Sanctuary' and Professor Keith Critchlow's magnificent lecture on the meaning of 'Temenos' as a sacred place, which wonderfully defied translation into text, this publication presents the lectures that were given in that series and the exhibition of photographs that supported it.

In a world that seems to have lost so much of that 'sense of the sacred' that was once our birthright, it seems to me that it is important that we find a place in our lives to reflect upon those matters of the heart that give true meaning to our lives; and that we are mindful of the need to rediscover the divine harmony that has been the teaching of wise men and women throughout the ages.

In a world that seems ever torn by conflict and discord, the theme of 'sanctuary' is especially important and, as these essays show, it can be expressed not only as an idea but also, in buildings and in gardens, as a form–the physical expression of Beauty, Truth and Goodness.

I commend to you not only this book, but also the work of the Temenos Academy. The name of 'Temenos' is itself an ancient word for 'sanctuary' and the Academy, like my Foundation, seeks to provide a place for reflection, study and true action in these uprooted times.

Contents

List of Illustrations

Introduction

DAVID CADMAN and JOHN CAREY

As His Royal Highness The Prince of Wales says in his Foreword, this collection of essays is based on a series of lectures given at his Foundation by the Temenos Academy during the academic year 2002–3. Not all the lectures could be translated into text and one essay has been added, but the theme remains — sanctuary within the great spiritual traditions.

It is, perhaps, ironic that a collection of essays on the form and meaning of sanctuary should begin by considering the Buddhist tradition, a tradition which, as Temenos Fellow Grevel Lindop observes, 'least clearly has a concept of sanctuary'. Nevertheless, the notion of 'refuge' is embedded in Buddhist thinking and it is this that the essay explores.

Sanctuary is much more clearly expressed in the Christian tradition and the next essay, by Richard Chartres, Bishop of London, explores the Christian vision of sanctuary and links it to the rebuilding of the church of St Ethelburga in London's Bishopsgate — a centre working for reconciliation and peace, a place of sanctuary reborn.

Tali Loewenthal, scholar and lecturer at the Department of Hebrew and Jewish Studies at University College London, then takes us on an ancient journey, back to the Temple in Jerusalem. He explores the Sacred Garden of Eden and 'the quest to draw the revelation of the Divine Presence back into the world, to re-create the Sanctuary'. Again and again he shows what 'sanctuary' has meant, and still means, in the Jewish tradition.

Supporting the lecture series was an exhibition of photographs by Gael Robertson, entitled *Breathing Spaces*. Much affected by the tragedy of 11 September 2001, Gael approached four places in the same part of London — a church of the Church of Scotland, a synagogue, a Roman Catholic church and an Islamic centre. She asked if she could photograph each of these holy spaces, on the basis that each would host the resulting collection of photographs and invite the other communities involved to share the exhibition with them. This imaginative act of reconciliation proved to be both inspiring and illuminating.

Emma Clark, who teaches at The Prince's School of Traditional Studies, takes us into the sacred garden of Islam with its pools and courtyards. In her essay, she tells of the meaning of sanctuary to the Muslim, of its importance to the spiritual path of Islam and of the way in which the garden helps in the constant remembrance of God. With examples drawn from her own studies, she also gives us guidance on the practical matters of design, the representation of the sacred on earth.

The essay by Kapila Vatsyayan, Fellow of the Temenos Academy and eminent Indian authority on sacred and traditional art, was not given as one of the lectures on which this collection is based. It is included as the editors felt that a contribution from the classical spiritual tradition of India was needed, and they were delighted when Kapila agreed to provide one. She paints a characteristically rich landscape of shrines, temples and places made sacred by worship, pilgrimage and prayer; and she embellishes these with the detail and meaning of ritual performances. The notion of 'sanctuary' is woven into the life of this tradition: 'Sanctuary is a journey from the ordinary mundane world . . . to a concentrated effort to see the unity behind the diversity of forms.'

Finally, it seemed right to include in this collection something about the Sanctuary that His Royal Highness The Prince of Wales built at Highgrove to mark the millennium. In their essay, Charles Morris and his colleague Mark Hoare, a former student at The Prince's Foundation, take us through the design and building of this sanctuary in a garden. And, acknowledging the inspiration and support of His Royal Highness to the Temenos Academy, of which he is Patron, and, of course, to his Foundation, it is fitting that the final essay in this book should be of his Sanctuary.

These are times in which there is a special need for the spirit of sanctuary to be felt and to be given place, and the terrible events that occurred in London on 7 July 2005, as this volume was nearing completion, make this clearer than ever. We hope that this collection will offer you matter for reflection — and, perhaps, inspiration also.

Acknowledgements

We would like to thank His Royal Highness The Prince of Wales for allowing us to use the photograph and drawing of his Sanctuary. We would also like to thank Charles Morris for permission to use the drawing.

We would like to thank the following for allowing us to use Gael Robertson's pictures of interiors of their buildings:

St. Columba's Church of Scotland, Pont Street, London SW1X 0BD
The Ismaili Centre, 1 Cromwell Gardens, London SW7 2SL
The London Oratory, Brompton Road, London SW7 2RP
The Westminster Synagogue, Kent House, Rutland Gardens, London, SW7 1BX

We would like to thank Rabbi Yosef B. Friedman for permission to show the photograph of Rabbi Yitzhak Schneersohn.

Buddhism and the Place of Refuge

GREVEL LINDOP

There is a certain tinge of the unexpected in beginning this lecture series with a talk from a Buddhist point of view. For of all the major world religions, it is probably Buddhism that least clearly has a concept of sanctuary. So if in this lecture I am to lay some kind of foundation for the series as a whole, then it is, as we shall see, likely to be a shifting and paradoxical foundation. Perhaps others will be able to solidify it. But in line, I think, with the Buddhist tradition, I shall be presenting a series of paradoxes and provisional statements and images which will lead, perhaps, not so much to a sense of security, as to what the late Alan Watts in the title of one of his books usefully described as 'the wisdom of insecurity'.[1]

The word 'sanctuary' of course means most fundamentally 'a holy place'; thence (I'm following the *Oxford English Dictionary* here) 'a place set apart for the worship of God or of one or more divinities'; thence in turn the *most* sacred part of any temple or church — the 'holy of holies'. Here already, by the way, we have the notion of a space within a space: the sacred temple which contains within itself a more central space, which somehow constitutes the essence of the surrounding building — as it were, the real temple within the apparent temple. (And it must be a universal principle that, within that, the ultimate temple is the human heart.) But sanctuary can also be, simply, a piece of consecrated

1. *The Wisdom of Insecurity* (New York: Vintage, 1951).

Facing page: Sima (boundary) stone, showing stylized Buddha's footprint; Chithurst Forest Monastery, Sussex, England

ground; and thence — by European medieval canon law but also, beyond and before that, by a universal human instinct — sanctuary comes to be a place where certain fugitives are immune from arrest. Beginning simply as a place of holiness, sanctuary thus comes to mean a place of safety.

In most modern societies the idea of a religious building as providing immunity from interference by the civil power has no legal basis at all, and this is perhaps just as well. But its intuitive, instinctive validity for most people remains nonetheless extremely powerful. Whatever the detailed rights and wrongs of the matter, for example, I don't think that many people, of any religion or none, could feel entirely comfortable about the forcible removal of the Ahmad family from the Ghausia Jamia Mosque in the West Midlands in July of 2002. Equally it could be argued that those who encouraged them to take refuge there were ill-advised. In either case, the point is that the episode shows that the practical application of the tradition of sanctuary, in this sense, is alive and well in the popular consciousness. It is a natural human instinct to feel that the exercise of force in a place dedicated to spiritual practice is inappropriate. And no one in this country is likely to be altogether unaware of the story of Britain's most prominent martyr, St Thomas à Becket, murdered in front of the altar in Canterbury Cathedral: an episode which has been built, as one of its cornerstones, into English literature from Chaucer to T. S. Eliot.

But already we have fallen into speaking of the theistic religions, of Christianity and Islam, with which, together with Judaism, much of this series will be concerned. Does any of this correspond to anything in Buddhism? Those who have had much contact with Buddhists may already know that the characteristic Buddhist answer to almost any question is 'Yes . . . and no'. Sanctuary, as we have seen, is first of all a holy place. Are there holy places in Buddhism? Well, yes and no. There are places of pilgrimage, there are places of spiritual practice, there are places set aside for certain religious procedures. All of them are special, all of them are treated with great respect, all of them can arouse joy in a properly attuned person who enters or contemplates them. But are they 'holy' (the Anglo-Saxon word) or 'sacred' (the Latin word)? Because Buddhism is not a theistic religion, its spaces and practices are not dedicated to a transcendent God. This is not at all to say that Buddhism is an atheistic religion, of course. All traditional branches of Buddhism, from the Theravada school of Sri Lanka and Thailand through to the Zen and Ch'an schools of Japan and China and the Tantric schools of Tibet, acknowledge an immense pantheon of gods. But these gods are, if you like, angels and archangels, benevolent spirits, an aristocracy of subtle and colourful beings who may have long lifespans but who are actually born and die like us, only to be reborn in the human world. Buddhists are perfectly happy to make offerings and recite prayers at their shrines: most houses in Thailand, and many office buildings as well, have outside a small shrine to the Vedic gods — those inherited from Hindu culture — where fresh flowers are put every day. But these are the minor actors on the Thai spiritual scene. The important business of the spiritual life is the progression by means of generosity, virtue and meditation towards enlightenment — freedom from rebirth and the suffering it brings, and the entrance into the deathless or transcendent state, Nibbāna, which lies beyond the realm of humans and gods alike. And this is the pattern typical of all Buddhist societies, and of all individuals and social groups that try to follow the Buddha's teachings. Life is a path: it leads either to rebirth or, for those who are ready, to liberation, Nibbāna, Nirvāna, the deathless, enlightenment, Buddhahood, call it what you will. But this goal is not thought of as a *god* and it is not personalized. Thus there cannot be things or places which are 'holy' or 'sacred' by virtue of being dedicated to a god.

So is nothing sacred in Buddhism? Obviously we have problems of translation here, but I would say emphatically that yes, certain things are sacred or holy. At this point I have to make it clear that I speak very much as a Western lay practitioner of Buddhism in the Theravadin tradition of Thailand. I believe that what I say will prove on the whole to be valid throughout all branches of Buddhism, but the details may vary a great deal and I would not presume to speak for any other tradition, nor even to speak as an expert within the Buddhism of Thailand. My perspective is that of a Western lay person, with the limitations which that must involve.

But let us return to the question: what is holy or sacred in Buddhism? In Theravada Buddhism the word equivalent, I think, to 'holy', and sometimes translated that way, is the Pali word *ariya*. More literally this may be translated as 'noble', but it is clear from the things to which it applies that it has to do with that which is spiritually pure or profound and complete. Hence it approximates as nearly as possible to the Christian notion of the holy, and it has sometimes been argued that 'holy' would be a better translation than 'noble'.

Those things in Buddhism which are invariably referred to as *ariya* are quite limited in number. They are the Four Noble (or Holy) Truths taught by the Buddha, which contain the essence of his teaching; the Noble or Holy Eightfold Path, which is the Buddha's detailed teaching on how to live and how to practise spiritual development; and the

Ariya Sangha, the Noble or Holy Community of those who have experienced liberation or enlightenment.

Let me expand slightly. The Four Holy Truths are, first, the Truth of suffering — that all existence involves some degree of suffering; secondly, the Truth of the cause of suffering — which is ultimately our craving, our desire for things to be thus and not otherwise; thirdly, the Truth of liberation from suffering — that there is a state of transcendent happiness available to us which is beyond our sufferings and discontents; and fourthly, the Truth of the Path — the way of life and spiritual practice which can lead to that happiness.

The Holy Eightfold Path is simply the fourth Truth — the Truth of the Path to enlightenment — explicated in more detail under eight headings which deal with the development of morality, meditation and wisdom. This Path becomes specifically 'holy' when, as it reaches completion, each of its eight aspects becomes fully developed as a mental attitude in those who touch the transcendent in such as a way that they will not fall away from it. But by extension, in a less perfect sense, the Path is one which anyone can tread to some degree.

Finally we have the *Ariya Sangha*, the Holy Community. This consists of those who have actually realized enlightenment — Buddhas, mystics, contemplatives, of whatever religion or philosophy, who have purified their hearts to the point of eradicating greed, hatred and delusion, and have entered into enlightenment and become freed from the round of death and rebirth. The conclusion that we have to draw from this is that what is essentially holy in Buddhism is either teachings — the Four Truths, the Eightfold Path; or people — the *sangha* or community.

Even then, it should be noted that no verbal formulation of Buddhist teachings can be ultimately 'holy' or *ariya*, since language itself is imperfect and temporary. All such formulations deserve respect, and may be venerated as pointing to an ultimate truth which is beyond words; but only that ultimate truth is actually holy. Similarly, whilst it behooves us to treat all our fellow beings with the greatest respect, and whilst (as William Blake put it). 'Every thing that lives is Holy', it would be odd to convince ourselves dogmatically that any given individual we might meet was ultimately sacred in a way that somehow exceeded the value of our other fellow beings. We should be mindful of the possibility that anyone we meet may be an Enlightened One now, or perhaps will be in future. But what is venerated is, really, a principle which lies beyond individual manifestation.

It would certainly be true also to say that *Nibbāna* or enlightenment is holy; but since this is unconditioned, absolute, beyond all worlds, essentially indescribable, and to be known ultimately only through the experience of it, to call it 'holy' doesn't get us very far. It cannot in itself be worshipped or venerated. In a sense, therefore, no geographical space — whether a temple, a place of pilgrimage, or a shrine — can technically be fully *ariya* or 'holy' in the Buddhist sense. This is not to say that it cannot be numinous, treated with immense respect, regarded as a special place in which spiritual experience is more likely, and so on. But equally, since in a Buddhist view the root of suffering is craving, and what is ultimately holy is the following of a teaching which leads away from craving, to treat any place or building as *ultimately* holy would be a self-contradiction.

I think that this fine balance of attitudes is best illustrated at this point by a little story. A few years ago I visited the International Temple near Ubon, in north-east Thailand. This is a monastery established by the great Thai meditation master, the late Achaan Chah, for the training and support of European Buddhist monks. I was given a tour by the abbot, who showed me the monks' own meditation hall, some distance from the public meeting rooms. The monastery was in the middle of tropical forest, and indeed the monastery lands had been enclosed deliberately to preserve the rain forest from destruction by logging or road-building, so that in recent years the monastery with its grounds had become an island of untouched forest amid much barer land. The meditation hall, a very simple building, was designed for maximum openness and ventilation, as well as to preserve the feeling of being in the forest, since these monks were forest monks who deliberately stayed far from urban centres. The hall had been designed by a German architect and its end wall, where the Buddha statue stood, was of handsome dark stone. The area for the monks to sit and practise was simply a flat platform floor, with a light roof supported on thin pillars. There were no walls as such, though cloths or partitions could be hung if needed. At some time in the decade or so since the hall was built, I was told, a small wild fig tree had seeded itself in, or beside, the one substantial stone wall, at the focus of the hall. By the time of my visit, the small wild fig tree had become a very large fig tree indeed. Its roots poured over the stone wall and flowed down it like huge silver serpents. The trunk was slowly engulfing parts of the wall like wrinkled silver candle-wax. The wall itself was tilting because the tree was starting to lift it from underneath. Contemplating this astonishing sight, I said to the abbot, 'Aren't you going to have to do something about that tree before long?' The abbot looked reflectively at the tree for a few moments and then said, 'Well, I don't know that we need to. It might be rather nice just to let it carry on and take its course.'

I suddenly realized what he meant. Why be especially attached to that wall? It wasn't actually supporting the building. To allow the tree to change it or even destroy it was a natural on-going demonstration of the truth of impermanence, a fundamental part of the Buddha's teaching. The symbolism was highly appropriate: the Buddha had advised his followers to meditate at the roots of a tree, or in a cave, or in any suitable place they could find. He hadn't told them to erect buildings; and he himself had attained enlightenment meditating under a wild fig tree. The wall posed no danger to anyone and was structurally separate from the roof. Why not let the tree have its way, and in the process remind the monks that they were supposed to be forest-dwelling mendicants, and teach them about impermanence and the folly of being attached to any material thing, including a building?

If we come back in this context to the question, 'In Buddhism, is anything sacred?' and take the term 'sacred' in a non-technical sense, then I think we have to say, yes, many things are sacred. Life is sacred, trees are sacred, the Buddha's teaching is sacred, those who try to practise it are sacred, those who do not try to practise it are sacred as well. But what is important is to realize, through the Buddha's teaching, that everything changes and nothing lasts. Not all churches, shrines or temples are grown over by trees. But one way or another they will all be gone in the end, and in that case where can we find true sanctuary— in the sense of both holiness *and* safety?

Let's approach the question from a different angle. I've already mentioned in passing that the International Temple was itself actually providing sanctuary in one sense for trees and for many other things by protecting an area of tropical forest from exploitation. This is a continuation of a very ancient practice whereby the grounds of Buddhist monasteries, where it would be deeply improper to take life, have traditionally been a place of safety for hunted animals and other stray creatures, wild and domestic, which are cared for and fed on left-over food. Throughout the Buddhist world the monasteries were also, and to some extent still are, as in medieval Europe, centres of social work, medicine and care for those of the elderly who have no family. In recent times a successful programme of treatment for heroin addicts has also been established at a well-known Thai monastery. In this broad sense the monastery or temple has always been a sanctuary, a place of refuge for the vulnerable of whatever age, class or species.

But despite the growth at times of large institutional monasteries in India, Tibet and elsewhere, the spirit of Buddhism remains very much that of the forest wanderer, and the main area of the temple grounds is not in itself actually 'consecrated' in any formal way. Yet there is one space which is important in Buddhism, and which is ritually established, and to be found in every Theravada temple or monastery where ordained monks or nuns meet formally together. This is the *sima*.

The *sima* is simply a boundary, within which formal acts of the *sangha*—that is, the ordinary community of Buddhist monks or nuns—can take place. As with many aspects of Buddhist tradition, there is a rich and intricate body of customs surrounding the *sima*, but essentially it is simply the agreed boundary around an area used for certain formal purposes. In theory its size can range from (as a minimum) an area just large enough for twenty-one monks to sit at forearm's length from one another, to (at a maximum) an area with a diameter of 48 kilometres, or in ancient terms three *yojanas*–a *yojana* being regarded as half a day's walk. The *sima* defines the most important area of the monastery or temple, within which the monks hold their monthly meeting to chant the rules of their order and within which the ordination of new monks would take place.

In ancient times *simas* could be defined by natural features such as a tree, a river or an outcrop of rock. Today most *simas* are roughly the size of a meditation hall, and very often they coincide with the boundaries of the meditation hall itself. At all events, the *sima* must have clear boundary markers; and in recent centuries these have normally taken the form of specially chosen stones called *nimittas* (the word means simply 'signs'). These could be any large stones, but most often they are carefully shaped spheres of stone made by a sculptor or craftsman. So that the *sima* may remain valid even if the monastic buildings are destroyed, the *nimittas* are often buried below ground, frequently under the floor of the shrine hall itself. This makes the boundary markers absolutely secure against disturbance but paradoxically means that they are no longer visible, and therefore smaller markers are normally placed on the surface to show the position of the real *nimittas* underneath. In forest monasteries, however, the *nimittas* are often kept deliberately simple and may simply lie on the surface.

At Chithurst Forest Monastery in Sussex, England, the boundary stones lie on the surface but are carved with the traditional emblem representing the Buddha's footprints. The elaborate and stylized footprints are in fact a very ancient symbol of the Buddha, descending from the aniconic period of Buddhism during its first six hundred years when the person of the Buddha was not represented at all. Since they also symbolize the quality of standing firmly based upon the earth, the device is especially suitable for a *sima* stone.

But any other device, including rough uncut stones, could have been used. The footprints used at Chithurst are simply a happy and creative embellishment of the stones.

The *nimittas* or boundary stones are normally positioned to define a rectangular area, one being placed at each corner of the *sima* (generally at the cardinal points of the compass), and one in the middle of each side (thus giving eight), with one more (a ninth) at the centre of the area itself. The stone at the centre, which in most monasteries is buried underground, is the focus of many customs and is felt to be of special symbolic importance. Whilst the placing of the other stones is simply accompanied with chanting by the monks to announce the establishment of the *sima*, the positioning of the central stone is usually the focus of much celebration and pomp. At Amaravati Buddhist Centre in Hemel Hempstead, England, the central stone — known in Thai as the *luk-nimit* — is a perfect sphere, to which for several months previous to the ceremony lay people applied offerings of gold leaf, so that it came to resemble a complete sphere of gold. When the *sima* was finally dedicated, the Princess Galyani Vadhana, the sister of the King of Thailand, performed the ceremony of cutting a ribbon which allowed the *luk-nimit* to drop into the pit prepared for it in the earth and thereby become the hidden symbolic centre of the space where the formal acts of the *sangha* could be carried out.

In this way the *sima*, whether a small one no bigger than the main hall of the monastery or a large one coinciding with the boundaries of the monastery grounds, has something in common with the Christian idea of consecrated ground. Especially interesting is the fact that a previously declared *sima* is in theory still valid, even if no one any longer knows that it is there. For this reason, establishing a new *sima* always includes a ceremony to abolish any previous *sima* which may have overlapped in any way with the same area. This is done even in countries like Britain where Buddhism has a very short history. For who knows whether in some remote unrecorded past the place might not have been declared a *sima* by some long-forgotten community of monks? You can't be too careful.

But is the *sima* a sanctuary? Rationally, no. But as a place of the numinous, as a spatial focus of the monastery, or just as a place where regular repeated acts of spiritual discipline are performed, it certainly has such a quality for those who practise in the appropriate tradition. Yet the magic which it may well have is not in any way codified, and its basic purpose is strictly practical. In the same way, other spaces which are important in a Buddhist context exist also for practical purposes. The shrine room or meditation hall — often two alternate expressions for the same thing — is simply a room, usually with a

Buddha statue or other suitable symbol — where people can practise meditation, make offerings of flowers, lights, incense or food, or chant and make spiritual aspirations. Such places are designed to be conducive to such activities, but in principle they could be done elsewhere. The space itself need not ultimately have special qualities. As noted earlier, it is not in the spirit of Buddhism to be dependent upon buildings.

As if to demonstrate this, those structures which do symbolize the ultimate in Buddhist aspiration are often ones that *cannot be entered at all*. The most familiar of these is probably the stupa.

The stupa is essentially a stylized burial mound, which may or may not contain actual relics. Ultimately it is a reminder of the burial mounds in which the remains of the Buddha's physical body were interred after his cremation. Its different levels or stages often have symbolic links with the four elements, the parts of the human body and so on, and it is of course also a representation of the cosmic mountain, the *axis mundi*. The tapering spire and finial, often gilded, indicate the aspiring path to the deathless, to *Nibbāna*. But you cannot go into it, and apart from venerating it and reflecting on its significance, the traditional way of relating to it physically is to circumambulate it, to walk around it clockwise once or thrice or any larger number of times. It is a sacred *structure* but not a sacred *space*, and in fact its whole object is to point to something which is beyond space. The process of circumambulation itself hints at this: for it is a journey which spatially goes nowhere, but which acknowledges a different dimension.

Other major Buddhist structures have a similar quality. Borobudur in Java, for example, the largest Buddhist architectural structure in the world, is one that might surely be expected to contain some kind of central shrine. But it does not. It is a giant mandala or contemplative diagram on many levels, around which and up whose various levels pilgrims were expected to walk in an approximately spiral path, reaching an upper level which symbolizes the highest levels of spiritual experience and the nature of Buddhahood itself. But the structures on the top terrace, including that at its centre, are stupas. The stupas contain Buddha statues. But the pilgrim cannot enter them. Not because the pilgrim cannot enter Buddhahood or enlightenment — far from it — but because the task of the stupas is to point beyond the spatial dimensions of this world altogether.

So where is sanctuary to be found? Well, virtually every occasion which involves Buddhist chanting begins with the recitation of the Three Refuges. Commitment to these, and sometimes the formal reciting of them, are often considered to be the specific, ritually defining marks of Buddhist commitment, in so far as such a mark is conceivable. Buddhists commit themselves to going for refuge to the Buddha, to the *Dhamma* (Sanskrit *Dharma*), and to the *Sangha*. In what sense is this possible, or even meaningful? The Buddha is of course the historical spiritual teacher, but also in this context the Buddha-mind, the transcendent enlightened consciousness itself. The *Dhamma* is first of all the Buddha's teaching. But it is also that teaching thought of as a making-explicit of cosmic law, of the way things ultimately are, with the assumption that our suffering arises from our failure to comprehend the true nature of things — a true nature which a real understanding of the teaching or *Dhamma* will reveal to us, thus ending our suffering. The *Sangha* here is specifically the *Ariya Sangha*, the noble or holy community of those — Buddhas, Bodhisattvas, saints, awakened ones — who have realized *Nibbāna* or enlightenment. But it also extends into an awareness of community in a wider sense — the community of those who attempt to follow the Buddha's path, the community of all who at one time or another wish their fellow beings well, the community of humanity as a whole, the community of all sentient beings — humans, deities, animals, *all*. Reciting or reflecting on the Three Refuges is thus in part a way of arousing faith or confidence. The Buddha has lived, and is in some sense still a timeless presence. The teaching is still available for our guidance. Others before us, suffering like us, have trodden the spiritual path and gone beyond suffering, experiencing the ultimate happiness of liberation.

The concept of refuge is thus not far from the theistic concept of faith or trust in God. And in fact it has a profound harmony with human nature. If we watch our own minds we can easily see that at moments of stress or anxiety we have a natural tendency to grasp at comforting thoughts, whether in the form of memories, cherished plans, other people whom we love, or favourite addictions or fantasies. In other words, going inward for refuge to something or other is normal human behaviour. The Buddhist perception is that if these are parts of the conditioned world, then however dear or useful they may be, they are ultimately temporary and will at last fail us. Only by developing the habit of turning to the timeless and unconditioned — to enlightenment, symbolized by the Buddha; to the ultimate nature of things and the right way of dealing with situations (*Dhamma*); and to the example of those who have embodied liberation in human form — can we find a secure foundation not subject to the ravages of imperfection and impermanence.

Clearly this is not altogether a different procedure from the summoning up of faith, and the practice of prayer, in other religious traditions. There is a notion in the Western world that Buddhism is a religion of self-reliance. But the truth is less clear-cut. Since enlightenment or *Nibbāna* is by definition unconditioned, we cannot make ourselves enlightened no matter how hard we strive to practise good conduct and to meditate. Ultimately enlightenment descends, as and when it descends: we can invite it but we cannot really deserve it. In this respect it resembles the Christian concept of divine grace. And in some Buddhist traditions — those mainly Far Eastern traditions known as the Pure Land schools–the teaching is that as conditioned beings, full of imperfections and hardly consistent enough to strive reliably through countless lifetimes to purify ourselves sufficiently to enter enlightenment by our own efforts, our best chance is to throw ourselves entirely upon the vow of one of the great Bodhisattvas, who have undertaken not to enter *Nirvāna* until all other beings have already done so. According to this school of thought, Buddhas such as Amida, existing in other world-systems of the immense cosmos, have established realms where we may be reborn and bide our time until through *their* merit, rather than our own, we may enter *Nirvāna*.

To attain rebirth in such a 'pure land', it is necessary to meditate on the Buddha or Bodhisattva in question, to recite prayers to him — in the case of Amida Buddha, Chinese and Japanese Buddhists use his name as a mantra repeated innumerable times. Of course, the relinquishment of self involved in putting total trust in the Bodhisattva, and the meditational practices of reciting the prayer or name and so on, become from one point of view simply another form of the usual Buddhist path. And it may be said that since from the Buddhist point of view the self or person as an absolute entity is an illusion in any case, the question of whether we reach sanctuary by own own efforts or those of another is ultimately merely a question of emphasis. We cannot, after all, reach enlightenment by the efforts of a self which never existed in the first place.

Yet subjectively it feels as if something strives to change, to learn, to meditate, to develop. It is probably in this sense that the Buddha uttered amongst his last teachings the famous words:

> Therefore, Ananda, you should live as islands unto yourselves, being your own refuge, with no one else as your refuge; with the Dhamma as an island, with the Dhamma as your refuge, with no other refuge.[2]

The words — handed down of course in Pali — are wonderfully rich and paradoxical. To

2. *Mahāparinibbāna Sutta, Dīgha Nikāya* II.100; see T. W. Rhys Davids, *Dialogues of the Buddha* (London: Pali Texts Society, 1977), II.108. I have slightly adjusted the translation.

begin with, it is not clear whether the Pali word *dīpa* should here be translated as 'island' or as 'lamp', and it's likely that a play on words is intended. Ideally, the follower of the Buddhist path is both lamp — source of vision or understanding — and island — place of security. Then, telling us to be lamps or islands and refuges to ourselves, with no other lamp or island or refuge, in the same breath the Buddha tells us to take the *Dhamma* as our lamp, island or refuge. This is resolved by the words which follow, which are less often quoted:

> And how does [one] live as an island unto himself, as a refuge to himself? Herein, one abides contemplating the body as the body . . ..[3]

He continues in this vein, and the instructions for the contemplation of body, feelings, consciousness and *Dhamma* are given. In other words, the *Dhamma* — the universal law or the teaching — is in oneself. Looked at rightly, one's own body, feelings and mind *are* the teaching and the way to liberation. To put it another way, the kingdom of heaven is within you. In this sense, you can certainly be your own refuge.

And when the *Dhamma* (which is built into one's own body, feelings, mind, experience) is fully understood, craving ceases and makes way for enlightenment, liberation, *Nibbāna*, *Nirvāna*. And it is of course *Nibbāna* which is, for Buddhism, the ultimate sanctuary: the unconditioned, the pure, the inexhaustible, the deathless.

Nibbāna is the ultimate sanctuary. Being timeless and beyond conditions it is impossible to describe, but according to a classic early Buddhist text, it is the ultimate happiness, entirely blissful and unmixed with anguish. It is 'the golden City of Nibbāna, the unaging, undying, peaceful, blissful, heat-assuaging and secure, which has been entered by many hundreds of thousands of Buddhas'.[4] As cool water allays fever, so *Nibbāna* allays the fever of defilements. As water quenches the thirst of men and beasts, so *Nibbāna* quenches the thirst of beings for sense-pleasures. It is like an antidote to poison; it drives out old age and dying; like space it is not born, does not age, does not die, and depends on nothing. One who realizes *Nibbāna* is like a man who escapes from a blazing and scorching fire to a place where there is no fire; he is like a man who has been entangled with corpses or covered with mud and slime, who frees himself from these things and comes into a clean and pure place. This is the true sanctuary. All others are only provisional.

Let's return here to a point made near the beginning of this talk. For Buddhism — as,

3. Ibid.
4. Commentary to the *Cunda Sutta, Satipatthāna Samyutta,* as quoted in Nyanaponika Thera and Helmuth Hecker, *Great Disciples of the Buddha* (Boston: Wisdom Publications, 1997), p. 50. The translation is Nyanaponika's.

surely, for other religious traditions — the true sanctuary can never be a building. The true sanctuary is beyond all places, and yet the path to it lies through the human heart. When we look at the spaces and the buildings which symbolize this, therefore, it is the provisional, the light and the fragmentary which prevail and yet which point to something beyond themselves. The Buddha advised his monks simply to meditate in the forests, in caves or at the roots of trees. In the Theravada tradition, monks attached to a monastery frequently spend much of their day alone in small wooden huts about the size of a garden shed in which, or near which, depending on the weather and the local insects, they can meditate for long hours. The huts are called *kutis*; they are the outward sanctuaries of these monks and their sheer fragility, temporariness and simplicity make them to my mind perfect examples of Buddhist architecture. They impose little, they demand little, they offer no protection but in that very fact they point to the sanctuary within.

Sanctuary in the Christian Tradition: St Ethelburga Bishopsgate

RICHARD CHARTRES, BISHOP OF LONDON

I sometimes wonder whether my family's distant origins in La Beauce, close to 'l'insigne basilique de Notre Dame de Chartres', are responsible for the scepticism which I have entertained, for as long as I can remember, regarding the proposition that we stand, here and now, on the very pinnacle of enlightenment. Can it really be true that we view matters from a standpoint so elevated above the common prejudices of mankind that we are competent to judge all other times and places? Could it be that we have something to learn from ancient traditions, like those informing the notion of sanctuary?

I was brought up at a time when the abolition of the sanctuary screen, and the multi-purpose worship space, were in vogue. It was clearly inefficient to set aside a dedicated space to represent a next-worldly dimension. We were told to admire churches that doubled as basketball courts. Altars had to be dragged out of their position in the east and placed in the midst of the church; and the Christian community was taught to worship the warmth that rose from proximate human bodies, rather than going on pilgrimage to the new dimension of the Kingdom.

I believe that this has led to the real absence of a sense of the infinite possibilities of heaven, and to a profound disorientation. The sanctuary has been evacuated and the blood supply to the symbolic life has been cut. In consequence, as the poet Robert Lowell puts it,

Facing page: Door handle from Durham Cathedral

In this small town where everything
is known, I see His vanishing
emblems, His white spire and flag-
pole sticking out above the fog,
like old white china doorknobs, sad
slight, useless things to calm the mad.[1]

Let us go back to fundamenta.

The scientific understanding of space as infinite expanse with no centre has little connection with living in a meaningful world. Human beings have never actually lived in the space conceived by mathematicians as isotropic, or having the same properties in all directions. The space experienced by human beings is oriented.

Space is not homogeneous for the person who is spiritually aware. Such a person experiences manifestations, like Moses in the book of Exodus. God called to him out of the bush and said, 'Draw not nigh hither; put off thy shoes from off thy feet for the place whereon thou standest is holy ground.'[2]

Sacred space is a revelation of what is real in the midst of the formless expanse. It reveals the fixed point, the pole, the central axis for orientation. In doing so it permits a cosmos, an ordered world to be constituted. In profane space there is no fixed point and no true orientation. There is no possibility of a cosmos — only the fragments of one, like the debris of a stellar explosion.

A universe comes to birth from its centre. Jesus Christ was crucified at Golgotha, the place of the skull. Whose skull? The skull was that of the first human being: Adam, made from the dust of the earth.

The lifting up of Christ on a tree in this central place in the history of human life provides the vertical axis to which the new humanity is drawn. 'As Moses lifted up the serpent in the wilderness, even so must the Son of Man be lifted up, that whosoever believeth in him should not perish, but may have eternal life.'[3] The Christian sanctuary then has a central vertical axis; an orientation towards the east, the next-worldly dimension of the divine kingdom; and a horizontal invitation, a space within which the new humanity is assembled and nourished.

This happens to be the festival day of St John of Damascus, a wonderful patron for our meditations on the Sanctuary. In his treatise *On the Incarnation and the Holy Icons*, he says this:

1. From 'Waking Early
Sunday Morning', in *Near the
Ocean* (London, 1967), p. 15.
2. Exodus 3:5.
3. John 3:14–15.

In former times God, who is without form or body, could never be depicted. But now when God is seen in the flesh conversing with men, I make an image of the God whom I see. I do not worship matter; I worship the Creator of matter who became matter for my sake, who willed to take His abode in matter; who worked out my salvation through matter.[4]

Idolaters worship matter.

Manichees hate matter.

Materialists are — ironically — indifferent to matter.

Christians give thanks and refer matter to the Creator.

I suspect that this reverence has to be continually re-appropriated, as we see the casual way in which people can contemplate destroying sanctuaries and eleventh-century churches to make way for further runways in Harmondsworth. We do this so light-heartedly because we have ceased to live in an oriented world, as conscious participants in a sacred cosmos, and instead treat matter not as bearing the divine signature but as mere stuff to be exploited by those who have themselves absurdly aspired to be gods.

Traditional sanctuaries, created in the beginning by the contagious character of holiness, became safe places, a refuge from pursuit and death that also promised a process of cleansing and a new beginning.

The sanctuaries of the ancient world, and one thinks of particularly celebrated ones like the temple of Diana in Ephesus, gave way in the Christian Empire to a proliferation of local sanctuaries often associated with the cult of the martyrs.

By the late fourth century, with a huge tide of the half-converted entering the now established church, many edicts relating to the abuse of sanctuary indicate that this had become a preoccupation of the imperial government. There was particular concern about the tendency of debtors to escape their creditors by taking sanctuary. (A picture of Enron executives taking refuge in the Crystal Cathedral rises before my eyes.) There was an attempt to abolish the right of sanctuary altogether in 398, but in the following year the tradition was definitively and legally recognized.

In 431 the area of sanctuary was extended to church courtyards and ancillary buildings, to provide somewhere other than the church building itself for the masses of fugitives to eat and sleep. The Empire was criss-crossed with a multitude of Sangattes, and the practice of taking sanctuary was increasingly regulated. In particular, all arms were to be left

4. Greek text in J.-P. Migne, *Patrologia Graeca* xciv.1245; trans. David Anderson in *St John of Damascus: On the Divine Images–Three Apologies Against Those Who Attack the Divine Images* (Crestwood NY, 1980), p. 23.

outside the sanctuary area; but, in case this tempted the pursuers to seize their quarry, the penalty for violating sanctuary was death.

About 600 the code of Ethelbert, the Kentish king who so hospitably received Augustine, provides the first mention of the practice in English law. Eventually a dual legal regime was developed in England, to reflect the balance between the spiritual and the temporal dimensions of community life.

Canon Law, the law of the Church, allowed the protection of sanctuary only for a limited period, to check blood vengeance and in order that some wergild compensation for injuries could be paid. In a number of English churches there was a stone seat beside the altar, called the 'frith' or peace stool, upon which the sanctuary seeker sat. One such still survives at Hexham, one of the great sanctuaries of the North. Often you had to advertise your application for sanctuary, and Durham Cathedral preserves a fine sanctuary knocker with which supplicants could announce their arrival. The fugitive then had to confess his crime to the clergy, giving full details. Thereafter he had to surrender his arms, swear to obey the house rules and pay the admission fee.

In Common Law, this spiritual space where the normal laws were suspended was recognised as an asylum for an accused felon, who could save his life by seeking sanctuary. If he then confessed his crime within forty days he was allowed to take an oath to abjure the realm. He was permitted a rather short time to journey to the nearest port, dressed in a white robe and keeping to the highway. During Edward III's reign in the fourteenth century, one abjurer was given only nine days to get from Yorkshire to Dover on foot.

There were two kinds of sanctuary by this point. General sanctuaries protected only those guilty of felonies. Peculiar sanctuaries established under royal charter also gave protection to those accused of petty and even of high treason. There were twenty-two such chartered sanctuaries in England, and here in the City of London there were two: at St Mary le Bow and St Martin le Grand. The most famous sanctuary in England was of course Westminster Abbey, given its privileges by a grant of Edward the Confessor. Dean Stanley wrote that 'The precincts of the Abbey were a vast cave of Adullam for all the distressed and discontented in the metropolis who desired according to the phrase of the time to "take Westminster".'

During the fifteenth century violations of sanctuary were not uncommon. Lollards were dragged from churches, since heresy was thought to have no rights. Edward IV, after the battle of Tewkesbury, had the Duke of Somerset and twenty Lancastrian leaders arrested in sanctuary and beheaded.

In 1540 there was a far-reaching reform of the practice, and seven cities of refuge were established after the Old Testament model—Wells, Westminster, Manchester, Northampton, York, Derby and Launceston. Manchester refused the honour and Chester was substituted.

In 1623, in an Act which marked a new stage in the subordination of the spiritual to the temporal power, sanctuary for criminal offences was abolished altogether throughout England. Sanctuary is a suburb of the City of God, a space within which the powers of this world do not hold ultimate sway. Its invasion was a further nail in the coffin of the medieval idea of the balance and distinction between the temporal and spiritual spheres.

Sanctuary lingered on however in civil processes. One notable example was Whitefriars, between Fleet Street and the Thames east of the Temple. Today it is recalled in the name of an inconsiderable side street, but this was the neighbourhood nicknamed 'Alsatia' in Shadwell's Restoration plays. Arrests in Alsatia were possible only on writs issued by the Lord Chief Justice himself. In 1697 all such alleged privileges were abolished.

One interesting survival which lingers on, however, is the immunity which MPs enjoy within the Palace of Westminster. They cannot be arrested or served with writs in the precincts, and this dates from the time when there was still a conviction that 'such divinity doth hedge a king' that a presumptive right of sanctuary attached to royal palaces.[5]

Sanctuary, however invaded by the state and surrendered by the church, has continued to resonate as an idea in the modern world. In the 1840s, the Sanctuary Movement in the United States organized an underground network which moved slaves from the plantations of the South to freedom in Canada and the North. Churches were important staging posts on the journey north, offering the fugitives sanctuary from unjust law and an imbalance of power.

The concept of sanctuary was once again invoked in the United States in 1982, by the Presbyterian congregation of the Reverend John Fife in Tucson, Arizona. They declared their church a sanctuary, a safe place from the prevailing policies of the Imperium. Their example was followed by hundreds of Christian communities in a new sanctuary movement, offering protection to refugees from Central America caught up in the overspill of cold war violence in places like El Salvador, which had already claimed the lives of Archbishop Romero and many others.

Europe too generated a sanctuary movement which opened churches to migrant workers and asylum seekers. In Manchester, which you will remember had declined the honour of

5. The information in the preceding twelve paragraphs has been drawn from the article 'Sanctuary' in the 11th edition of the *Encyclopaedia Britannica*, 28 vols (Cambridge, 1910–11), xxiv.129–31.

being one of Henry VIII's seven cities, the Bishop and the present Dean of Ripon offered sanctuary to Viraj Mendes who claimed to be in mortal danger if he was returned to his country of origin, Sri Lanka. Very recently we have witnessed the Bethlehem siege, and seen asylum seekers taking refuge in a church near the camp at Sangatte. There may be no legal justification for claiming sanctuary rights, but in the present media climate state authorities are cautious about invading holy ground, calculating that there is enough contagious divinity left to provoke an outcry against them should they use violence.

Now of course as the very notion of a sanctuary was under a cloud in the churches in my youth, popular opinion had a surer grasp on the essence of the thing albeit in a somewhat demotic form. If you asked a representative sample of Londoners about 'sanctuary', they would say it is a place where women go to have a facial, a leg wax and a sauna in Covent Garden. This debased survival of ancient names also makes the Priory into a place where celebs go to dry out between binges. There is, however, a certain continuity with its ancient roots in this consumerist version of the concept. The Sanctuary in Covent Garden is a place where women go to escape from the pressures of men, money and make-up. There is a desire for refuge from a hostile, confused environment, although the aim is beautification and pampering rather than moral renewal. Sin and redemption have taken rather autistic forms.

The church of St Ethelburga Bishopsgate is one more example of the tenacity of the concept of sanctuary. This ancient church was torn apart by violence. It was reduced in 1993 to a heap of rubble. A man was killed at the threshold, and there was a fifteen-foot crater outside the door. Some advocated the development of the site as office accommodation, with a patent glass façade on Bishopsgate to enclose the ruined arcade which survived the bombing. I was actually told by one of the architects of this scheme that 'young people these days' do not like to see explicitly Christian symbols. He seemed to think that hearing the words should be communication enough with the Divine Word. I was unconvinced; but I received a battering from the utilitarians and the bottom-liners, and my determination to rebuild the sanctuary was regarded as backward-looking folly.

I telephoned Cardinal Hume and reported that I had been contemplating the rubble. It had come to me that we ought to rebuild the sanctuary of St Ethelburga as a centre where people could practise and make peace in a place scarred by the evidence of what happens when the peace of God is shut out of the world. I said that in view of the religious dimensions of the conflict which had manufactured the bomb, it was important that we should rebuild as a partnership of Christians in order to serve all people of faith and good will.

A priest with a greater caution and addiction to due process would have said, 'Well, Richard, it is an interesting idea but you have so many. I shall certainly discuss what you have said with my advisers.' Fortunately the Cardinal was not of that kidney and he said immediately, 'That must be right. We should do it.'

'And let them make Me a sanctuary that I may dwell among them.'[6] That is what we have done at St Ethelburga in Bishopsgate. To the west, there is a great door opening on the world of the concrete canyon that Bishopsgate has become. There is no patency but there is a squint, so that people, passers-by, can glimpse another possibility within in a building which is as strongly oriented as it always has been. It is a place for people to assemble, a place with a low threshold and a welcome for seekers of all traditions; but there is also a sanctuary, with the vertical axis and the table to gather the community, and steps up to a next-worldly dimension.

Thanks to the work of many friends and to a marvellous team, the sanctuary is now renewed and the St Ethelburga Centre under its new Director Roland Smith has already begun its work of reconciliation and peace. I am grateful to have been given the opportunity to share in this labour, which has served to revive yet another ancient theme: the link between the concepts of sanctuary and diplomacy. Diplomacy used to have a divine dimension, and the office which I hold as Dean of the Chapel Royal was especially concerned with the making and ratifying of treaties. In the British Museum there is preserved a seventeenth-century engraving of my predecessor as Dean, Launcelot Andrewes, at the high altar of the Chapel Royal administering an oath on the Vulgate on the conclusion of a treaty between England and Spain.

It would be easy to dismiss all this as whimsy from the muniment room, but my intuition is that we are overdue for a re-balancing of the temporal and the spiritual. The relation between our exploration, as human beings, of the outer spaces and our inner spaces is as intimate as breathing in and out. Our achievements in outer space, first exploring our globe and now even reaching to the stars, have been extraordinary. For two centuries past, hope has been resident in political processes and in the faith that a heaven on earth could be created by education and social engineering. We have seen huge advances. Some of the

6. Exodus 25:8.

world's growing population experience a standard of security, health and prosperity never before attained in human history. Only a fool would decry these achievements.

At the same time, the sanctuaries only rarely seem to give access to energy or greater reality. They are apologized for and allowed to survive because they make a measurable contribution to tourist revenues. David Jones has spoken of the evacuation of the sanctuaries in his *Anathemata*, the greatest long poem in English of the twentieth century:

Ossific, trussed with ferric rods, the failing numina of column and entablature, the genii of spire and triforium, like great rivals met when all is done, nod recognition across the cramped repeats of their dead selves.

Then he talks of the priests,

these rear guard details in their quaint attire, heedless of incongruity, unconscious that the flanks are turned and all connecting files withdrawn or liquidated — that dead symbols litter to the base of the cult-stone, that the stem by the palled stone is thirsty, that the stream is very low.[7]

Jones knows however that there is an underground river which flows and which can be discovered. Now that hope is migratory once more and people wonder whether there really is salvation in technology; now that the distress of the earth is more obvious, and the consequences of seeing ourselves not as participants in a sacred creation but as master exploiters of mere matter have become clearer — now it may be that the doors of the sanctuary can be opened once again and we can bathe in 'the dearest freshness deep down things', and receive the energy which flows from the Beyond-All. I hope so. I believe so.

Let the last word be with Eliot, the poet and sanctuary warden:

Of all that was done in the past, you eat the fruit either rotten or ripe.
And the Church must be forever building, and always decaying, and always being restored . . .
The Church must be forever building, for it is forever decaying within and attacked from without;

7. *The Anathemata: Fragments of an Attempted Writing* (3rd ed.: London, 1972), pp. 49–50.

For this is the law of life; and you must remember that while there is time of
   prosperity
The people will neglect the Temple, and in time of adversity they will decry it . . .

I have loved the beauty of Thy House, the peace of Thy sanctuary,
I have swept the floors and garnished the altars.
Where there is no temple there shall be no homes,
Though you have shelters and institutions . . .
When the Stranger says: 'What is the meaning of this city?' . . .
What will you answer?[8]

8. T. S. Eliot, *The Complete
Poems and Plays 1909–1950*
(New York, 1952), pp. 101, 103.

Sacred Garden, Sacred World:
The Sanctuary in Jewish Teaching

TALI LOEWENTHAL

The Jewish Sanctuary, the site of the Temple in Jerusalem, has been a focus of faith for millennia. But the theme of Sanctuary both precedes the Temple and also succeeds it, in the sense that although the Temple in Jerusalem may be in ruins, there are other aspects of the Temple which are eternal. The broader concept of the Sanctuary in Jewish teaching leads us back to the past, to the very beginning of time: the Creation of the world, and Adam and Eve in the Garden of Eden. Eden itself is described by the Jewish Sages as a form of Sanctuary. We will consider the Sanctuary built by Moses, described in the Hebrew Bible, and explore the idea that the physical Sanctuary was complemented by changes in the way in which people related to each other, and the idea of a Sanctuary in the heart. The Sanctuary of Moses led to the Temple of Solomon in Jerusalem, and then to the Second Temple, destroyed by the Romans over nineteen centuries ago. Despite that, for Jews its site retains its sanctity, as the focus of prayer and the point where the spiritual realms and our physical universe meet. We will also briefly look ahead, with a vision of the future of all humanity, which can be seen as depicting the Sanctuary writ large: not only a sacred Garden, but an entire sacred world.

Facing page: Model of the Second Temple standing in the grounds of the Holyland Hotel, Jerusalem

THE TEMPLE IN JERUSALEM

The key to the spiritual Sanctuary is the physical one, because in Jewish teaching the goal is to reveal the Divine in this physical world. The Temple in Jerusalem is the focus of Jewish daily prayer, both because the Jews face the Temple when they pray and also because the prayer services mirror the services in the Temple. Much of the Jewish teaching in the Mishnah and Talmud is directly focused on it.[1] One tractate of the Mishnah provides details of the design of the Second Temple, which the older Sages of the Mishnah had seen themselves;[2] and many pages of Jewish traditional teaching discuss the ways in which it functioned as the spiritual and legislative centre of the Jewish commonwealth.

After the destruction of the Temple the ultimate site of pilgrimage for the Jews has been the West Wall, the last remaining section of the outer perimeter of the Temple. Observers have called this the 'Wailing Wall', because the Jewish pilgrims would weep at the destruction of the Temple and pray with yearning for it to be rebuilt. Indeed, this longing is a constant refrain in Jewish prayer throughout the world. However, the prayer for the rebuilding of the Temple does not have to be accompanied by tears, nor does it concern only the Jewish people. To understand this we need to consider the spiritual purpose of the Temple and Sanctuary in Jewish thought. This is a different kind of exploration. A few words are necessary as to the sources which are being used.

SOURCES AND METHOD

The ideas in this paper are drawn from successive layers of Jewish thought. The core text is the Hebrew Bible. However, this is viewed through the prism of the Sages of the Talmud and Midrash, and through the further perspectives of the Jewish mystical tradition and contemporary Chassidic teachings. Some of the ideas presented here derive from a particularly significant Chassidic discourse, written in New York in 1950 by Rabbi Joseph Isaac Schneersohn, the sixth Lubavitcher Rebbe, shortly before he passed away.[3] This discourse was seen by Rabbi Joseph Isaac's followers as his last will and testament, and as bearing a spiritual message relevant to the world. It begins with the words 'I have come into My Garden', citing the Song of Songs (5:1), and was frequently discussed by the seventh Lubavitcher Rebbe, Rabbi Menachem Mendel Schneerson (1902–1994). In order to approach this teaching about the nature of the Sanctuary, we will also encounter

1. The Mishnah was compiled by Rabbi Judah the Prince in northern Palestine 1800 years ago and records the teachings of earlier Sages. The Talmud (the word means 'study') is an extensive commentary on the Mishnah, compiled over several centuries in two versions, one in Palestine and the other in Iraq (Babylon). The Babylonian Talmud was completed around 1500 years ago.

2. This is Tractate Midot (literally: 'Measurements'). Hillel (d. 10) and his contemporary Shammai, leading Sages of the Mishnah, both lived in Jerusalem in the latter period of the Second Temple, which was destroyed by Titus in the year 70.

3. The Hebrew text of Rabbi Joseph Isaac's discourse is in Book of Discourses, Bati LeGani (Kehot Publication Society: New York, 1977) pp. 1–26, followed by further discourses on the same theme by Rabbi Menachem Mendel Schneerson. An English translation is Bati LeGani 5710 (SIE: Brooklyn, 1980).

Image of Rabbi Joseph
Isaac Schneersohn

other ideas from the Sages of the Talmud and from the Jewish mystical tradition, in particular the thought of Rabbi Shneur Zalman of Liadi (1745-1812), author of the *Tanya*, a basic work of Jewish spiritual teaching.[4]

THE BEGINNING

'In the beginning, G-d created the heaven and the earth.' The opening words of the Hebrew Bible obviously refer to the beginning of everything. However, the Jewish Sages give us in addition to this a further text, something written between the lines or before the lines. The beginning of physical existence, of our vast cosmos, is a certain stage of Creation. It is neither its absolute beginning, nor its end.

The process of Creation began before the physical cosmos came into being, and also continues throughout time, from hour to hour and from second to second, as the Infinite Divine pours an endless stream of life-giving energy into the worlds in order to make them continue to exist and to give them life. The moment of Creation reported in the Hebrew Bible is the moment when this stream of energy began to form the physical universe, with its vast spaces, its stars, sun and planets, the 'heaven', and the actual large globe of rock with fire in its core and water and seas and land masses, the earth.

However, there were also earlier stages of Creation when *spiritual* universes or 'worlds' were formed. These continue to exist, as the luminous domain of spiritual reality which is concealed by our physical world. It is interesting to note that the Hebrew word for 'the world', or 'the universe', *ha-olam*, has the same consonants as the term for 'concealment': *he-elem*. Only the vowels have changed (and in Hebrew, vowels are a secondary aspect of the word, often not recorded). This verbal correspondence expresses the basic idea that the universe is a concealment of the Divine.

Now, are our physical world, and our physical life in it, merely a hiding and concealment of a deeper spiritual reality? Is the task of life therefore chiefly the quest to pierce the concealment and discover the radiant reality beyond, and thereby to reconnect with the Source of all? And is a Sanctuary a place where through reflection and prayer one reaches beyond this life to G-d above? According to Jewish teaching, this is indeed part of the quest, it is an important element of human experience, and it is one which is of constant and repeated significance. But there is a further aspect, and it is at this point that we begin to approach the Garden and the Sanctuary in Jewish teaching.

4. This work is most accessible in *Lessons in Tanya, the Tanya of R. Shneur Zalman of Liadi*, elucidated by R. Yosef Wineberg, translated by R. Levy Wineberg, 5 vols, (Kehot Publication Society: New York, 1987); or in Adin Steinsaltz, *Opening the Tanya* (Jossey-Bass: San Francisco, 2003).

The goal is that this opaque physical world should serve a function apart from that of concealing the spiritual beyond. This world is a realm where some important aspect of the Divine—perhaps the most important—can be revealed; a domain where, contrary to expectation, the Divine can 'dwell'. Thus the ancient Jewish Sages declared: 'The Holy One, blessed be He, desired to have a dwelling in the lower world'.[5] In an unfathomable way, there is something extra and unique that is achieved through this Divine dwelling in the world. To try to explain this, Chassidic teachers use the metaphor of the nature of light. When it is bright daylight, one does not appreciate 'light' to the same extent as when a candle is burning in a dark room at night. In the total gloom, suddenly and surprisingly illuminated by the candle, one appreciates an extra dimension of light, a quality of its beauty and of its most essential nature, which would not be apparent by day. The Divine dwelling *in this world* is like the candle shining in the darkness, somehow revealing more of the infinite Essence of the Divine than can be manifested in upper, spiritual realms. This Divine indwelling in our physical world is the Sanctuary.

What does this mean? Surely, G-d is by definition *omnipresent*, G-d is everywhere, so what do we mean by saying that He desired to dwell in our physical world? Surely He is already here in our world from the very beginning of time?

Yes, the Transcendent aspect of G-d is indeed everywhere: in our physical world of woe, in ethereal spiritual realms, and also utterly beyond all existence. However, while G-d is One, the Hebrew Bible and other Jewish teachings employ several different Names for the Divine. Some of these Names or terms for the Divine refer to the exalted Transcendent Oneness, the Infinite, *En Sof* in Hebrew, which is beyond all and everything and is also everywhere at once. This infinite Oneness is beyond time and all being. That is the transcendent aspect of the Divine.

Yet there are also other Names for G-d. One is the *Shekhinah*, the Divine Presence, that aspect of G-d which *shakhen*, literally 'dwells' or perhaps 'should dwell'. And where G-d dwells—there is the Sanctuary. One Hebrew word for Sanctuary is *Mikdash*, from the word *kadosh* 'holy': a holy structure. Another, which occurs many times in Exodus, is *Mishkan*, again from *shakhen* 'to dwell', meaning precisely this: the place of dwelling, the place where the Divine dwells.

Now, to speak of the Divine Presence as dwelling in the upper, spiritual realms seems almost a tautology. In fact, however, the spiritual realm is in Jewish thought not identical with the Divine, for ultimately the Divine transcends *all*, both physical and spiritual

5. Midrash Tanchuma, Naso, 16.

realms. However, by definition, that which is spiritual is at least in some measure *transparent* to the Divine radiance. In the upper spiritual worlds the Divine is *revealed*.

Quite different is the question of the Divine Presence dwelling in the lower, physical world of concealment. The lower world is, in general, opaque to spirituality, unless we work very hard to transform it.

It is specifically in this finite, physical, lower world of concealment that Infinite G-d desired to dwell: His *Shekhinah*, His Divine Presence, would dwell here, at the same time bonding with the infinite Essence beyond. So G-d created the physical universe, comprising the physical cosmos and our planet, as in the words quoted above from Genesis: 'In the beginning, G-d created the heaven and the earth'.

ADAM AND EVE: IN THE DIVINE IMAGE

The completion of the work of Creation was the moment when Adam and Eve were formed, and were placed in the Garden of Eden. One of the key concepts in the Hebrew Bible is the idea that Adam and Eve were created in the Divine Image. Since G-d is without form, this is another puzzling concept. One way in which it is explained is that within each person there is a structure of inner essence, mind and heart, leading to speech and practical action. This structure provides the framework for the constant multiple interaction between the soul, the body, other people, the wider environment, and G-d. The ancient Kabbalists tell us that this human inner pattern of essence, mind, heart, speech and action is in some way related to an infinitely exalted spiritual structure expressed by the Divine.

Indeed G-d has no form, yet the Hebrew Bible speaks of attributes such as G-d's Love and G-d's Severity. Thus the Kabbalists through the ages speak of the Divine Essence, the Infinite, and then of Ten Divine Attributes. Some relate to the Will and the Mind, others to the Heart and to the power of Action. They are aspects both of the way in which the Infinite is revealed to us, and of the chain of processes which lead to Creation.

These attributes are also expressed in the inner spirituality of man and woman. This is the Divine Image within a human being. In everyday ethical terms, it means the ability to reason, to speak, to act and to choose with inner freedom to fulfil G-d's Will. The point of free will within a person, enabling him or her to relate to and to express the Divine, is the deepest level of their individual Divine Image.

Now the Biblical story of Creation relates that not just one individual was created, but two, male and female. The Sages explain the subtlety of the Hebrew text by telling us that Adam and Eve were at first one person: a Janus-formed, hermaphroditic figure, male and female back to back, Adam on one side, Eve on the other.

Then G-d divided this dual form, so that one side was formed into Eve, as a separate person, and the other remained Adam, now a single individual. Rashi, the eleventh-century French Jewish Bible commentator, explains that the Hebrew word *tzela*, which we usually translate as 'rib', also means 'side'.[6] G-d took one side of the dual form and closed its back, thus fashioning Eve, and likewise closed the back of the other side, which was now Adam.

Why is this detail important for us? Because the nature of man and woman is crucial for the Jewish concept of the Sanctuary. The fact that Adam and Eve begin as a unity, are divided but then—ideally—regain that unity, will help us to understand not just the Sanctuary in the Garden or in Jerusalem, but the Sanctuary in the home and the Sanctuary in the heart.

THE DIVINE PRESENCE IN THE GARDEN

Adam and Eve were in the Garden of Eden. The Sages tell us that with them was the Divine Presence, the *Shekhinah*. The Garden of Eden was the first Sanctuary, because there G-d dwelt in the physical world, together with the human beings, Adam and Eve, created in the Divine Image.

When the Divine Image in the person is whole and is revealed, meaning that the person is connecting to the Divine with his or her innermost essence, thought, feelings and action—then the person himself or herself *is* the Sanctuary. The Sages explain this in a comment on G-d's words to Moses in Exodus 25:8: 'And let them [the Israelites] make Me a Sanctuary, that I may dwell among them.' The Hebrew word for 'among them' (*betokham*) can also be translated 'within them'. The Kabbalistic and Chassidic Sages call attention to this double meaning, and say that the existence of the Sanctuary implies that the Divine Presence dwells within each individual.[7]

What was the task of Adam and Eve in the Sanctuary of the Garden? 'To work it and to guard it' (Gen. 2:15): to engage in positive action in order to connect the world with G-d, and to refrain from negative action which might spoil or weaken that connection. Adam

6. Commentary to Genesis 2:21.

7. Thus states the sixteenth-century Kabbalist Elijah de Vidas, in his *Beginning of Wisdom*, 'Gate of Love', chapter 6, sec. 19. See *Bati LeGani* (as in note 3 above), chapter 1.

and Eve said to the animals and the world around them: 'Come, let us worship G-d Who created us!'; and they answered, 'The L-rd is King!'[8]

This is the perennial task of the Priest in the Sanctuary: to help others, and indeed the whole world — human, animal, vegetable and mineral — to connect with the Divine. The point of connection is not only human or earthly recognition of the Divine but also, as a further step in the same direction, submission to the Divine Will. This is the supreme task of human beings who, unlike nature, have been given free will and the choice of submission or rejection. Humanity also bears a pivotal relationship to all other material existence. When the Priest in the Sanctuary, Adam-and-Eve, submits to the Divine Will, then the entirety of existence connects with the Divine Essence and becomes its earthly expression. The 'world' as such becomes itself the idyllic Garden of Eden — because Adam and Eve connect to and obey the Will of G-d.

However, as we know, there came a calamity. There was a desire which was not controlled, a desire which was expressed in an action which broke the link with the Divine Will and therefore led to disaster for all material existence. G-d had forbidden Adam and Eve to eat from the Tree of Knowledge. The precise reason for the Divine command is not the issue. The very nature of such a command is that it emerges from G-d beyond our human understanding; and our submission to G-d is based on acceptance beyond reason.

As we know, Adam and Eve succumbed. The immense desire to be like G-d,[9] rather than to submit to Him, led to the step of eating from the Tree of Knowledge, defying G-d's command.

The result was twofold. On the one hand, Adam and Eve, and future humanity for millennia, were banished from the Garden. On the other, the Divine Presence was hidden from the world. The Garden of Eden had been the Sanctuary on earth, and now the Divine Presence had retreated from the world. The Garden of Eden continued to exist, but as an aspect of the *spiritual* realms.

Thus, on account of the first transgression of humanity, the radiance of the Divine Presence was hidden from this physical world. In effect, the earthly Sanctuary was destroyed. Then came another negative step: the first murder. Cain killed Abel, because of a jealousy which arose over the worship of G-d. When Abel brought an offering, G-d turned to him. His brother Cain was jealous that he did not enjoy the same closeness with G-d, and killed him. The result was that the world became yet more dark. The Divine Presence retreated yet further, to an even more remote level of the spiritual realms.

8. Psalms 95:6, 93:1; Pirkei deRabbi Eliezer 11.
9. See Genesis 3:5.

What was happening? The Presence of the Divine means that the Divine Will is revealed. Men and women live in such a manner that their inner Divine Image is radiant. They are connected with the Divine at the most profound level of their being; and this connection is expressed through their thoughts and their speech, and above all through their actions.

According to Jewish teaching, the actions which connect man with G-d are defined as the Seven Noahide Laws: the seven laws for the whole of humanity around the globe, who are all descended from Noah.[10]

These laws, which are by and large expressed in most religions, are: to recognize the unity of G-d; to be aware of the Divine in all that transpires and therefore not to blaspheme; not to murder, which includes concern for those unborn and for the aged and terminally ill; not to steal, but to be ready to give charity; not to commit adultery or to succumb to other sexual temptations; not to eat a limb from a living animal or to be wantonly cruel in other ways; and to set up a system of justice and spiritual education.

The Jewish Sages give a list, step by step, from the eating from the Tree of Knowledge onwards, of seven major transgressions on the part of humanity which led to the utter distancing of the Divine Presence from the world. Some time after Cain killed Abel, idolatry began. There was the violence before the Flood; and the Tower of Babel, defying G-d, after it. There was the civic evil of Sodom and the sexual immorality which pervaded ancient society. The world was dark.

Drawing the Divine back to the World

Now comes a new stage in existence, a new venture: the quest to draw the revelation of the Divine Presence back into the world, to recreate the Sanctuary. It starts with Abraham and his wife Sara, who rediscovered monotheism together and taught it to those around them some 3700 years ago. Then G-d told them to 'go to the land which I will show you',[11] namely the Holy Land—in order, ultimately, that there should be the Sanctuary and a nation of Priests ministering in it, in order to draw down a blessing for all humanity. In the Bible's words: 'Through you will be blessed all families of the earth'.[12]

After Abraham came Isaac, then Jacob, then the generation of the Twelve Tribes, then their sons and grandsons and finally the generation of Moses. Each generation succeeded in drawing the Divine Presence a little closer to the world. In the seventh generation after Abraham there was Moses.

10. They were listed and expounded in the twelfth century by Moses Maimonides in his *Mishneh Torah*, Laws of Kings, chapters 8:10–10:12, based on Talmudic explanations of the implicit meanings of a number of Biblical texts. See also Chaim Clorfene and Yakov Rogalsky, *The Path of the Righteous Gentile: An Introduction to the Seven Laws of the Children of Noah* (Targum Press: Jerusalem, 1987), and Shimon Cowen, *Perspectives on the Noahide Laws: Universal Ethics* (Institute for Judaism and Civilization: New York, 2003).

11. Genesis 12:1.

12. Genesis 12:3.

The Sages tell us that 'all sevenths are precious'.[13] The Hebrew Bible refers to the special qualities of the seventh day, the Sabbath, and the seventh year, the Sabbatical year. In the diagram of the Divine Attributes, taught by the masters of the Kabbalistic and Chassidic tradition, the first three relate to the Mind, and the lower seven to the heart and to practical action. The seventh of this group of Attributes is called 'Kingship', and expresses the idea of fulfilment in tangible action. In short, the seventh means 'completion'.

Hence the fact of being the 'seventh' gave Moses an extra degree of spiritual power. He was able to complete the task of drawing the Divine Presence back into our realm of physical reality, a task which had been begun by his ancestors.

The key moment when this began to be accomplished was the Theophany at Mount Sinai. The Divine Presence was revealed at the Mountain, as a source of holiness and as a source of Law. As we saw in the Garden of Eden, in order for the Divine Presence to dwell in the Sanctuary the Divine Will must be expressed, which is another way of saying that the Divine Law should be observed. At Mount Sinai, G-d's Will was revealed in the form of the Ten Commandments.

The *Zohar* and Chassidic teachings tell us that at that all-too-brief moment of revelation, the world itself became transparent to G-dliness at the foot of Mount Sinai.[14] Hence Deuteronomy (4:35) states that at that moment the Israelites 'were shown, so that you will know, that G-d is the Supreme Power, in heaven above and on the earth below—there is nothing else'. The Sages explain, firstly, that the Divine Voice emanated from every direction, all around them; and also that the Voice and the thunder which could be heard, were also *seen*: in truth, the doors of perception opened and the Divine reality of all was disclosed.[15] Mount Sinai, and the large camp of the Israelite people around it, became the Sanctuary, the Divine dwelling in this world.

Obviously, in a Sanctuary we would expect people's feelings towards each other to be filled with love. It is interesting to note the comment of Rashi, the eleventh-century French Jewish Bible commentator, that from the moment the Israelites camped at the foot of Sinai, even before the revelation, they felt spiritually unified, even though on many other occasions there were squabbles and arguments. This unity is reflected in a detail in the Hebrew text. When it says in Exodus 19:2 that 'the Israelites camped by the mountain', the singular form *va-yihan* is used rather than the plural, *va-yahanu*. This means, says Rashi, that they were like one person 'with one heart'.[16] Thus in their preparation for Divine Revelation they attained a unity befitting the Sanctuary, the dwelling of the Divine in this world.

13. Midrash *Leviticus Rabbah* 29:9.
14. See *Tikkunei Zohar*, section 22; *Tanya* I, chapter 36.
15. See Rashi's commentary to Exodus 20:15.
16. Rashi to Exodus 19:2.

Building the Physical Sanctuary

Then comes another step: the construction of the Sanctuary proper, the actual portable physical structure described in the Book of Exodus, built while the Israelites were still at the foot of Mount Sinai. The thirteenth-century Spanish Jewish scholar Nachmanides states that the Sanctuary described in the Bible is actually a kind of replica of Mount Sinai at the moment of the Theophany. Just as the Divine Presence was revealed on the Mountain, so it was revealed in the Holy of Holies in the Sanctuary. Just as G-d spoke to Moses on the Mountain, so G-d spoke to Moses in the Sanctuary. Just as Divine Law emanated from G-d's teachings on the Mountain, so Divine Law was expressed by G-d's instructions in the Sanctuary.[17]

Unlike Mount Sinai, however, the Sanctuary was portable. As the Israelites travelled through the desert, they took it with them. Wherever they camped, the Sanctuary was erected. Eventually, when after forty years they entered the Holy Land, they set up the Sanctuary at a place called Gilgal, later at Nob, Gib'on, Shiloh and finally, in David's time, it was brought to Jerusalem and erected there. Then David's son Solomon replaced the portable tent-like Sanctuary in Jerusalem with the First Temple made of stone, about 2900 years ago. This was destroyed in 586 BCE by Nebuchadnezzar and then, seventy years later, it began to be rebuilt as the Second Temple.

However, this is running ahead. Let us return to the earlier time of Moses, and consider the Sanctuary constructed at the foot of Mount Sinai. The details of its construction are in Exodus, its use and inauguration are in Leviticus, and the way in which it was central to the camp of the Israelites is described in the Book of Numbers. This latter point is a good place to begin. The Sanctuary was physically in the centre of the Israelite 'camp', its entrance in the east and the Holy of Holies in the west. Near the entrance of the Sanctuary were the tents of Moses and Aaron, who were both Levites. They were on the east of the Sanctuary. Near the three other sides, south, west and north, were camped three groups of Levites, descendants of the three sons of Levi. The Sanctuary was therefore surrounded by a rectangular perimeter of Levites. The Sages call the area within this perimeter 'the camp of the Levites', while the actual Sanctuary is termed 'the camp of the *Shekhinah*', the Divine Presence.

Then in an outer perimeter, again at each of the four points of the compass, the Israelites were grouped in four blocks, each comprising three of the Twelve Tribes of

17. See Nachmanides' commentary to Exodus 25:1; and also Exodus 25:22, Leviticus 1:1 and Numbers 7:89, with Rashi's commentary on each verse.

Israel. This area is called 'the camp of Israel'. On account of the Sanctuary in the centre, this entire area had an aura of holiness. We should also bear in mind that there was a constant Pillar of Cloud by day, and a Pillar of Fire by night, focused on the central Sanctuary area, as a direct expression of the Divine Presence.

Now let us proceed towards the Sanctuary. There was an outer Courtyard, in which was the Altar, with a long slope leading to its top. Then there was a low structure with walls of upright cedar wood planks overlaid with gold, set in silver sockets at their base, and a complex canopy with woven tapestry fabric on the inside and an outer layer of fur.

This structure included the Outer Sanctum, where there was a small golden Altar for incense and the seven-branched golden candlestick, the Menorah; and then behind a tapestry curtain there was the Inner Sanctum, the Holy of Holies. In the Holy of Holies was the sacred Ark, a chest of cedar wood overlaid both inside and outside with gold, and the carved *Kerubim*—rendered as 'Cherubs' in the standard English translations, and explained as two forms, one male and the other female, with wings.[18]

Within the Ark were the Tablets of Stone which Moses brought from Sinai, on which were engraved the Ten Commandments. The Sages tell us that they were actually made of sapphire. This ultimate expression of the Divine Will and Divine Law was the inwardness of the Sanctuary, in the golden Ark in the Holy of Holies. Only once a year, on the Day of Atonement, would anyone enter this inner Sanctum. On that day, while the whole of Israel fasted, the High Priest would enter, with a pannier of incense. This event, together with other aspects of the lengthy service in the Sanctuary on this day described in Leviticus 16, signified G-d's granting atonement to the Jewish people for their sins; this atonement is now made through the repentance, fasting and prayer in the synagogue.

INAUGURATION OF THE SANCTUARY: ENTERING THE GARDEN

The moment when the Divine Presence began to dwell in the physical Sanctuary constructed at Sinai is described in Leviticus 9:24. The Sages tell us that this moment is also the theme of a passage in Solomon's Song of Songs.

A long Jewish tradition, going back to Rabbi Akiva in the second century, explains this as a song of Divine Love—love emanating from G-d, and love directed to G-d. A key verse reads: 'I have come into My Garden, My sister, My bride' (Cant. 5:1). The lover has come into the Garden to be with his beloved.

18. Zohar III 59a.

According to the Sages of the Midrash, these words refer to the moment when the Divine Presence was revealed in the Sanctuary at Sinai.[19] The Sanctuary is the 'Garden' of the Divine, and it is the later expression of the Garden of Eden. The Sages describe the process which has been outlined here — how the Divine Presence was in the Garden, with Adam and Eve, but departed because of a series of sins, and then was drawn back by a dynasty of seven righteous figures, seven generations. Moses was the seventh — 'and all sevenths are precious' — and he succeeded in drawing the Divine Presence back into this physical world, in the Holy of Holies in the Sanctuary. At that moment the Divine Presence re-entered the Garden of the Sanctuary.

But, we may ask, how far does the Garden of the Sanctuary extend?

SANCTUARY-COMMUNITY

When we consider the Inner Sanctum of the Sanctuary we sense the infinite purity and holiness of the first Sanctuary, the Garden of Eden. From this inner point of purity there extend successive perimeters, where the holiness is of diminished intensity yet still tangible: the Outer Sanctum, the Courtyard, the camp of the Levites, the camp of the Israelites.

The ancient Jewish concept of a Sanctuary is of an Inner Sanctum where the Divine Presence is revealed, and also of a *community*. In the camp of the community there is holiness. Hence we are told in the Hebrew Bible that certain individuals have to wait outside the Camp. A notable example is a person suffering from *tzara'at*, described in Leviticus 13–14. This means a condition in which the skin turns white. The word is often inaccurately translated as 'leprosy'. The Sages state that this was a mystical disease which afflicted a person who spoke evil concerning others. Thus in Numbers 12 we read of Miriam being afflicted with *tzara'at* on account of having spoken critically about her brother Moses. The one with *tzara'at* dwelt outside the camp until the condition cleared. This cure meant, say the Sages, that he had repented of his transgression of speaking with the evil tongue.[20]

The ethical ideal of the ancient Jewish Sanctuary is that people should be as one, like one person with one heart. Those who offend against this have to dwell outside the camp, temporarily, till they are able to come to terms with dwelling with others, with love.

19. Midrash Rabbah Cant.5:1.

20. See Babylonian Talmud, Erkhin 16b; Rashi to Leviticus 13:46; and Rabbi Menachem Mendel Schneerson, *Torah Studies* (Lubavitch Foundation: London, 1986), pp. 184–6.

SANCTUARY-FAMILY

Another aspect of the Community-Sanctuary is the family. When the Israelites are counted, as they frequently are in the books of Exodus and Numbers, it is 'by their families'. It is at this point that we return to the theme we encountered in the Garden of Eden: that husband and wife begin as one, at some supernal spiritual dimension. Then they are divided, by virtue of their birth in different families, and then they rejoin and create their own family together.[21]

This unity relates also to the Divine Image in humanity. In the pattern of Divine manifestations which the Kabbalists describe, there are both a male and a female dimension. The effulgence of the exalted transcendent level flows downwards in, so to speak, a male fashion, and is received and expressed by the Divine Presence in this world, the source of the feminine. These twin dimensions of the Divine are also expressed in the very heart of the Sanctuary: in the twin cherubs, one male and one female, which face each other above the sacred Ark in the Holy of Holies.

This theme of holiness is expressed in marriage, whence the pure and sacred joy at a traditional wedding. 'When a husband and wife succeed together, spiritually,' say the Sages, 'the Divine Presence dwells between them.'[22] They cite the Hebrew words for 'man' and 'woman': *iysh* 'man' contains a *yud*, the first letter of the Tetragrammaton, the Holiest of Divine Names; and *ishah* 'woman' has a *heh*, the second letter. In addition, both words also contain the word *esh* 'fire'. It can be either a positive flame of joy and holiness or a negative conflagration of uncontrolled and unfocused passion. Through wholesome marriage, the Divine is revealed.

At the domestic level of the Community-Sanctuary, the family in their home represent the Divine. Their unity, harmony and love manifest holiness.

THE SABBATH

In traditional Jewish life the key time for the gathering of the family in the Sanctuary of the home is on the Sabbath and on Festivals.

The Hebrew Bible repeatedly states that work is forbidden on the Sabbath and on Festivals, but does not provide an explicit system explaining how 'work' is defined. It is interesting that the Mishnah and Talmud define 'work' in terms of the building of the

21. See Zohar I 85b.
22. Babylonian Talmud, Sotah 17a.

Sanctuary at the time of Moses. Those activities which were required to cut the wood, weave the tapestries, and all else which went into the construction of the Sanctuary, are forbidden on the Sabbath.[23]

Why? Because, say the Chassidic Sages, on the Sabbath the Sanctuary is complete. Our daily work in the six days of the week is in fact constructing it, and on the Sabbath it is whole.[24] Hence work is forbidden; to engage in any of the activities required to construct the Sanctuary would suggest that it is not yet complete, and the sense of the Presence of the Divine in the Sanctuary of the home and the world would be disturbed.

Another important aspect of the eternal Sanctuary in Jewish life is the daily prayer service, which corresponds in a number of ways to the service in the Temple. Certain physical features of the Temple — particularly of the Second Temple — are mirrored in the appurtenances and layout of the synagogue, which since Ezekiel has been called the 'Small Sanctuary'. Thus the *bima* (platform where the Torah is read) in the centre of the traditional synagogue parallels the Altar in the centre of the Temple Courtyard, and the separate raised women's gallery corresponds to a temporary gallery for women constructed annually in the Second Temple during the Tabernacles festival.

CRITICISM

At all periods, the atmosphere of the Sanctuary of wood or of stone has to aspire to genuine spirituality, and this sense of holiness must also be matched by a similar standard in the life of the individual, the family and the community. When this was not achieved, Prophets such as Isaiah railed at the populace, asking rhetorically: without adherence to these personal spiritual values, what does G–d care about all your offerings?[25]

The external must be matched by the internal, the observance of laws between man and G–d must be matched by observance of those between one person and another. Over the millennia, complaints similar to that of Isaiah have been heard time and again, such as those of the Chassidic movement which began in the eighteenth century.

THE CORE: LOVE AND HOLINESS

Thus from the Inner Sanctum of the Sanctuary one moves outwards: to the Priests who administer its service, to the individual home and the community which, ideally, is

23. Babylonian Talmud, Shabbat 73b.

24. This relates to the idea that the Sabbath 'has the quality of the World to Come' when the Sanctuary-Temple will be rebuilt. See Babylonian Talmud, Berakhot 57b.

25. See for instance Isaiah 1:11.

dedicated to expressing its values. At the core of these is the command in Leviticus 19:18: 'Love your neighbour as yourself.'

The Jewish Sage Hillel, in the first century of the Common Era, and later Rabbi Akiba in the second, declared this to be the essence of Jewish teaching. 'This is the whole Torah, the rest is commentary,' said Hillel. 'This is the great principle of the Torah,' said Akiba.[26]

Beyond the immediate community around the Sanctuary there is the broader, non-Jewish society. The Hebrew Bible repeats many times the command to love the stranger. Further, Jewish thought maintains that a non-Jew who observes the Noahide Laws can achieve the highest spiritual goals: he or she attains the level of the righteous, and inherits the world to come. Thus while the Priesthood of the 'Kingdom of Priests' directly carries out the service in the physical Sanctuary, ultimately all humanity, created in the Divine Image, participates in the broader Garden of existence, the indwelling of the Divine in the world.

WHAT CAN DISTURB THE GARDEN?

Here we see the sacred Garden: the Sanctuary and the community around it, and the wider global society, where the Divine dwells in individuals, in families, and ultimately in all humanity. All, potentially, are of one heart.

Is there anything which threatens the peace and harmony in the Garden of the Sanctuary? Yes. The animal in the heart of man. Violence, greed, cupidity, self-seeking—sometimes, indeed, wrapped in apparently gentle garments, yet animal nonetheless. The Chassidic Sages tell us that people have different kinds of Evil Desire. In one it is like a forceful bull; in another a sly and lecherous goat. In another it seems harmless like a sheep but is in fact self-seeking and unthinking, timid when it comes to a real moral challenge.

The power of the Sanctuary is that it can transform the animal in man. The violent bull is brought to the Altar, where its energy becomes an offering to G-d. The bull in man is transformed and becomes sacred. So too the goat and the sheep. Their animal energy meets the Divine Fire on the Altar and is transformed into sacred energy. This is one of the secrets of the offerings in the Sanctuary and in the Temple in Jerusalem, as explained by the Chassidic Sages.[27] Through the service in the Sanctuary—whether the Sanctuary built by Moses or the Sanctuary in our own heart—violence is transformed into peace,

26. See Rashi's quotation of Rabbi Akiba's comment in his commentary on Leviticus 19:18, and Babylonian Talmud, Shabbat 31a. See also Rabbi Shneur Zalman of Liadi's *Tanya* I, chapter 32.

27. See *Bati LeGani* (as in note 3 above), chapter 2.

cupidity into holiness, complacent lack of concern into passionate commitment for the well-being of the world.

THE WHOLE WORLD AS SACRED GARDEN

The Sanctuary of the Pentateuch was the physical embodiment of one stage of the Jewish concept of Sanctuary, clarifying the basic theme. As described earlier, the portable Sanctuary built at the foot of Mount Sinai was brought into the Land of Israel and eventually became Solomon's Temple in Jerusalem, known as the First Temple. Solomon's speech at the dedication of the Temple (I Kings 8) makes it clear that this Temple, administered by the Jewish Priesthood, is for the benefit of all humanity (see verses 41–3). The Sages tell us that, from the Temple, blessing and forgiveness came to the whole world. During the festivals at the beginning of each year, seventy offerings would be brought— corresponding to the seventy core nations of the world, and eliciting Divine blessing for them.[28]

The First Temple was however destroyed, by Nebuchadnezzar. It began to be rebuilt seventy years later under the aegis of the King of Persia, and became known as the Second Temple. In its final stage it was enlarged by Herod. In the year 70 of the Common Era this Temple too was destroyed, and the Jews await the coming of the Messiah who will rebuild the Third and final Temple. As mentioned in the Book of Daniel (6:11), their prayers are always directed towards Jerusalem. Indeed, the heavenly, spiritual version of the Temple exists today: it is only its physical manifestation on the Temple Mount of Jerusalem that needs to be rebuilt. Yet that step is crucial.

What will happen then? According to the Jewish Sages, the sacred community around the Sanctuary in the desert of Sinai, the sacred Garden we have attempted to describe, will be translated into society throughout the world. 'House of Jacob, go, and we will accompany you, in the light of G–d,' say the nations according to Isaiah (2:5).

All men and women will observe the Seven Noahide Laws, and will in their inner being experience the holiness which is the essence of all existence. Marriage will be wholesome and healthy, children will again feel themselves to be part of unified families. It will be a moment when all war will seem totally senseless, and when the technology of weaponry will be utilised instead for food production, adequately feeding the billions of the world: 'They will beat their swords into plough-shares, and their spears into pruning forks;

28. Babylonian Talmud, Succah 55b.

nation will not lift up sword against nation, and they will no longer learn war' (Isaiah 2:4).

How will we reach this time? How can we transform our world of woe into a sacred Garden, the community of the Sanctuary? Maimonides, a Jewish scholar living in Egypt eight centuries ago, speaks to us as follows: 'A person should always consider that he is equally balanced between good and evil, and that the world is equally balanced between good and evil. If the person does one good deed, he tips the balance for himself and for the whole world to the side of goodness and salvation.'[29]

Rabbi Menachem Schneerson advises us that in our remarkable epoch, with a level of scientific and technological development unparalleled in the history of humanity, we have the power to draw the Divine Presence into the world and to reveal our globe as a sacred Garden, where each heart and each home is a Sanctuary, unified by the tangible Sanctuary of Jerusalem.[30]

29. Maimonides, *Mishneh Torah*, Laws of Repentance 3:4.
30. See *Bati LeGani* (as in note 3 above), vol. 1, pp. 224–33.

The Westminster Synagogue, Rutland Gardens, London

How? Through acts of goodness and kindness, following the prescription of Maimonides. Through our daily positive actions we can, each one of us, bring redemption to the world, revealing its beauty as Garden and Sanctuary. Then indeed G-d will again say, as in King Solomon's Song of Songs: 'I have come into My Garden.'

Breathing Spaces

GAEL ROBERTSON

FOREWORD

Breathing Spaces was a non-profit-making arts project initiated by Gael Robertson in the wake of the terrorist attacks that took place in the USA in September 2001. She approached four spiritual spaces in the Knightsbridge area of London (the Ismaili Centre, the London Oratory, St Columba's Church of Scotland and Westminster Synagogue), and invited them to share in her vision of a photographic exhibition exploring the notion of sanctuary provided by each of their buildings. Within one month, she began making the artwork and raised sufficient sponsorship to cover the project's production costs. In May 2002 the project was successfully launched at the Ismaili Centre before being hosted by each of the participating spaces in turn. Evening events invited members from each community to come together and enjoy an opportunity to be shown around each other's spiritual home. The overwhelmingly positive response from the communities to this, as well as to the exhibition itself, proved to be both inspiring and illuminating.

In October 2002, at the invitation of Professor David Cadman, *Breathing Spaces* was exhibited in the Alberto Vilar Gallery at the Prince's Foundation, where its exploration of spirituality and architecture seemed particularly appropriate.

Facing page: The London Oratory, Brompton Road, London

The artist would like to acknowledge the financial support of the project sponsors and to thank the participating communities who welcomed this opportunity to explore the way in which they relate to their own and their neighbours' architectural space and traditions.

SEPTEMBER 2001

Like many other individuals, and artists, I felt an overwhelming impotence in the face of events where the immensity of the tragedy was equalled only by the complexity of the cause. I knew I wanted to respond in some way and decided to attempt to create something practical, something positive, something arising from my own immediate urban geography. In conceptualizing what form this might take I constantly returned to the devastating photographic images of the destruction of buildings and lives in New York that were incessantly repeated and, I felt, after a certain amount of time, became both voyeuristic and divisive. I had the idea to counter in some way these images using the same medium of photography to construct, not destroy, and to heal rather than to hurt. I wanted to create images of strong peaceful architectural spaces that enrich and nourish life, that acknowledge the common threads connecting communities of different religious traditions and that encourage links between them.

I approached four spaces in the Knightsbridge area of London in which people of different faiths find spiritual focus, solace and strength: the Ismaili Centre, the London Oratory, St Columba's Church of Scotland and Westminster Synagogue. Each building provides a 'breathing space' in the midst of a hectic urban environment. Each provides a place of refuge, strength and peace in the midst of ongoing global conflict and irresolution. Breathing Spaces is a positive acknowledgement that these buildings and their communities co-exist peacefully a few minutes' walk from one another, yet also recognizes that there was little regular contact between them. I felt it to be an important time to initiate such links at a local level and chose to use a photographic exhibition as a focus for this.

The exhibition consisted of seven photographs taken in each of the four building interiors. In many traditions seven is the symbol of both creativity and completion. The resulting twenty-eight images were brought together to create a single exhibition that was hosted by each building and community in turn.

Each of the architectural interiors is simultaneously grounding and uplifting, its walls

St Columba's Church,
Pont Street, London

defining a sense of enclosure that is reassuring to those within. Yet these same walls necessarily make a division of space contributing to a sense of exclusion. Members of each participating community regularly passed by each other's buildings yet rarely dreamt of entering if they did not 'belong'. This is felt to be transgressing a boundary at some profound level, as well as raising anxieties about not knowing the 'right' protocol. This project invited people into each other's space, often for the first time — initially through the photographic images of their neighbours' architectural interiors, and subsequently through the opportunity to visit the exhibition as it was hosted by each neighbouring building in turn.

STILLNESS

In the immediate aftermath of 9/11, each of the communities that I approached had noticed not only an increase in numbers attending communal worship but also in those wishing to come and spend time peacefully reflecting alone in the space. This renewed my resolve to explore the particular quality of stillness that we both seek and find in specifically dedicated spaces.

The process of creating still images is itself concerned with communicating the intangible quality and atmosphere — or essence — of a particular space and time. It was important to me that the practice of the project mirrored the intent. An integral part of my approach was to spend a significant amount of time in these spaces before starting to make work there. In doing so, it became apparent that a sense of stillness and peace can be silently, yet powerfully, communicated through the combination of architectural space and light. I became increasingly interested in the transformational potency of the physical architectural interiors and how they relate metaphorically to the interior space or soul of the individual. *Breathing Spaces* was interested in this capacity for stillness, and the dynamic and often profound relationship that exists between the external, visible, material world of the public buildings and an individual's internal, invisible, private spirit.

LIGHT

Facing page: The Ismaili Centre, Cromwell Gardens, London

This then informed how I was going to work. I decided to be as little intrusive as possible in order not to disturb the very atmosphere I was trying to capture and convey in the

work. With the emphasis on the spiritual quality of light, it was important only to make photographs with available natural light and not to supplement this with flash or artificial lighting. *Breathing Spaces* developed over a period of eight months. Spending time watching the passage of light moving gently across the four different spaces, I became acutely aware of shadows shortening and lengthening as low level, winter sun penetrated deep into areas untouched in the later spring months. I was literally aware of witnessing an evolving 'calendar of shadows'. This was itself very inspiring and involved careful planning to be in the right place at the right time, having anticipated where the light would fall. It is this fleeting and intermittent nature of light that invests it with such a powerful sense of privilege. The resulting images use both extreme lighting contrasts—pools of deep shadows punctuated by strong shapes of sunlight—as well as softer, more gentle contrasts to communicate the way light literally shapes and animates these spaces. In the exhibition, the presentation of some of the images in large free standing light-boxes further emphasized the quality of spirituality inherent in the way that light operates in the four spaces.

DETAIL

As I spent time in each space, so I became increasingly focused upon architectural details and the way in which these themselves articulate different beliefs.

The choice of organic or geometric pattern, the selection of materials, the way in which light has been concealed or enhanced, all contribute to the sense of coherence within and between each of the buildings. It is the cumulative details of architecture and design that together create a single unified whole. *Breathing Spaces* further extended this relationship between each part and the whole to suggest that the buildings are each part of their respective communities and that these are in turn all part of a far broader community, both within London and beyond.

I deliberately did not label the photographic images as they were seen in the exhibition, the intention being to challenge people's preconceptions of different faiths and their complacency regarding their own. I wanted to encourage them to return and look again at their own space. Part of the project's aim was to challenge the way in which we are often too busy to 'see', literally and metaphorically. The project recognized how easily we slip into looking carelessly at a familiar place—or indeed people or ideas—feeling that we already know them, and our opinions of them, well. Whilst there were sufficient easily recognizable images, which people could feel comfortable with and identify as representing 'their' space, I also included a number of photographs that showed an unusual design detail or perspective, which viewers were often surprised to find was in their own building. In addition, the selection of photographs also tried to reveal how the four spaces relate to one another, encouraging the viewer to see the connections as well as the differences between faiths — for example, three of the four do not believe in figurative representations, and this is clearly reflected in the decoration of their buildings and thus in the photographs of them.

St Columba's Church,
Pont Street, London

COMMUNITY

Breathing Spaces recognized that each building functioned as a busy centre of activity, administration and support to its community as a whole. Each space is structured to run to its own rhythm, its own calendar of prayer times and holy days. However, I chose through the photographs to make explicit moments in which the community's presence

St Columba's Church,
Pont Street, London

is only implicit. There is often some evidence of habitual human activity: seating to be filled, candles to be lit, rituals to be observed. Nevertheless, there is a sense in which the space is peacefully waiting, caught between things that have happened in the past and will happen again in the near future. Human figures were deliberately excluded from the images in order to encourage a sense of intimacy and immediacy. The viewer was not to be distracted by focusing on others occupying the spaces they were looking at, but rather to feel that they themselves were 'in the picture'. Such direct engagement between the viewer and the space depicted provided an opportunity to 'enter' the neighbouring buildings and occupy all four spaces in turn, a gentle way of momentarily standing in one another's shoes — or not, in the case of the Ismaili Centre — of experiencing one another's sacred place.

AFTERWORD

Standing back two years after the launch of this project, I feel somewhat surprised that it happened at all. Perhaps it was to do a little with the climate of the months immediately after those first US terrorist attacks of 2001, when individually and collectively we were searching for an understanding of the 'other' as a partial means of making sense of events beyond our comprehension. This rendered the majority receptive to any invitation towards exploring, sharing and participating. *Breathing Spaces* was a challenging and rewarding project, a critical success that received favourable reviews — but, most importantly, one that in a small way attempted to create on a community level what we all hoped might happen on a global level. Whilst this moment may have passed in certain respects, essential connections remain between the communities who engaged with the project and the photographic images themselves retain a certain power and resonance. I could not have hoped for more. Whilst developing further projects I still receive comments from those who have stumbled across *Breathing Spaces* afresh, and whom it has touched. The way in which creative work can have a continual long term impact is for me encapsulated in the image of the beautiful fountain on the Ismaili Centre's roof garden, with ripples of clear water constantly moving outwards into the light.[1]

1. A catalogue of *Breathing Spaces* can be obtained by contacting Gael Robertson at ggorvyrobertson@mac.com

The Islamic Garden as Sanctuary

EMMA CLARK

Essentially, the word 'sanctuary' means a holy place: it comes from the Latin *sanctus*, meaning 'holy', and indicates a space set apart for the worship of God. It also has the meaning of 'protection, shelter and refuge' (literally 'immunity from arrest'), as well as that of a private retreat. Interestingly, one of the many words used to describe the Gardens of Paradise in the Qur'ān is *ma'wā*, which means 'refuge' or 'shelter': they are called *jannāt al-ma'wā*, the 'Gardens of Refuge' or the 'Gardens of Shelter'. Bearing this in mind, there can be no doubt that the Islamic garden on earth, inspired as it is by the descriptions of the paradisal Gardens in the Qur'ān, merits — to a certain extent — the term 'sanctuary', depending on how rigorous we are in defining the word. If we are strict with the definition — i.e. that it indicates a space set apart specifically for worship — then we will need to qualify 'sanctuary' more fully if we are to apply the term to the Islamic garden. We will see as this paper progresses whether such a usage can be justified.

It should be remembered that in Islam a worshipper can pray anywhere — as anyone who has travelled in the Islamic world will have seen. Muslims pray on the streets, in the area outside a mosque if the mosque is too full, in a park, at one's place of work, perhaps an office or schoolroom — and of course at home, almost anywhere in the house which is clean, although the lucky ones will have a room (a *zawiyyah*, literally 'corner') set aside for

Facing page: Pool in front of the Partal Palace, the Alhambra Gardens, Granada

the purpose of prayer and meditation. Indeed, in London I have seen Muslims praying in Hyde Park and, recently, on some grass by the Embankment, as well as inside the Houses of Parliament in the Moses Room next to the House of Lords. In all these cases the worshippers would, if possible, have a prayer rug, a small area which separates the place of actual prayer from the surrounding area. This area is, in essence, a sanctuary since it marks off a specially designated space for prayer; and therefore a prayer rug is, by its very nature, a kind of portable sanctuary. (The travelling Sufis in the past would carry no possessions except a rolled-up prayer rug and an ablutions jug.)[1] If no prayer rug is available then the area can be purified with water and words of consecration, thereby also creating a sanctuary, albeit of a rudimentary sort.

A sanctuary is thus an area which is outside of time and place. As Titus Burckhardt writes, 'Spiritually speaking, a sanctuary is always situated at the centre of the world and this makes it a *sacratum* in the true sense of the word.'[2] It is a place where the worshipper, on entering (or stepping on to a prayer mat) is one step closer to Heaven, and in a certain sense his individuality is submerged—or rather elevated from such and such a man to 'man as such'.[3] He is centred within himself, before God, humbly asking the Divine Peace to descend into his soul. As Burckhardt also writes, the sanctuary is the sacred art *par excellence* of sedentary peoples since the Divine Spirit, 'which is invisibly present in the universe, will "dwell" in the sanctuary—be it a temple, church or mosque—in a more direct and "personal" sense'.[4] So, although a primitive sanctuary can be made for a nomadic way of life (for example through water and prayer as mentioned above), a 'proper' sanctuary for settled peoples must be built to a traditional form. Why is this so important? Because every form manifests a certain quality: that is, there is a sacred symbol attached to every form and to alter this at whim would alter the meaning of the symbol and destroy the thread which ties us to Heaven.[5] The earthly form of the sanctuary, when built to the correct canonical model, is a reflection of its Heavenly archetype; this will be explained more clearly in relation to the Islamic garden as we proceed.

'Peace', *Salāam*, is the only word spoken in the Gardens of Paradise as they are described in the Qurˁān. This peace is promised to 'those who believe and do deeds of righteousness'. As the Qurˁān says of Paradise: 'There hear they no vain speaking nor recrimination. [Naught] but the saying "Peace, [and again] Peace"' (LVI:25-6).[6] So what does this really mean, the Peace that is promised to the righteous? Is it peace from the world or is it, as is said in Islam—more specifically, in Sufism—peace from our own souls? There is a famous

1. The Sufis are the more 'spiritually minded' Muslims who adhere to Sufism, the inward or mystical dimension of Islam.

2. Titus Burckhardt, *Sacred Art in East and West*, trans. Lord Northbourne (Bedfont, Middlesex, 1967), p. 17.

3. This is of course not 'gender specific'; 'man' refers to a human being, male or female.

4. Loc. cit.

5. The word 'religion' derives from the Latin *religio*, originally meaning 'bond' or 'fastening'—that is, religion is the link which ties us to Heaven. 'Tradition' derives from the Latin *traditio*, designating the handing down of beliefs, teachings and laws from a Divine source, usually orally. Thus, when speaking of a 'traditional form' in art or architecture, the meaning is that its source is ultimately from Above.

6. Qurˁān, LVI:25-26. All quotations from the Qurˁān are taken from A. J. Arberry, *The Koran Interpreted* (London, 1955), unless otherwise specified.

story of a disciple who complains to his spiritual Master, 'My wife has got the better of me,' to which the Master replies, 'It is not she, but your own soul that has got the better of you.' So the search for peace on earth, which is a foretaste of the peace which we will be given in the Heavenly gardens, is not just peace from the world but, more importantly, peace from our own soul (*nafs*): and this is not the immortal soul, but the passional soul, the ego and all its desires. The greater *jihād*,[7] *al-jihād al-akbar*, is, according to a saying of the Prophet, the war with our own souls. The longing for contentment and serenity of soul is like a vague memory of our primordial state before the Fall when man was at peace with his Creator and therefore at peace with himself and his neighbour. In order to regain this primordial paradisal peace those seriously committed to the spiritual path (*aṭ-ṭarīqah*) need to reach a state of constant remembrance of God (*dhikr Allāh*).

And what role can the Islamic garden play in this journey? Well, like all sacred and traditional art, its beauty can be an aid in drawing the visitor closer to God. More particularly, the four-fold form of the traditional Islamic garden on earth, usually known as a *chahār-bāgh*,[8] is a reflection of the four gardens (or more specifically 'two pairs' of gardens) described in the Qurʿān (Chapter LV). These are both the inspiration and the archetype of the beautiful traditional Islamic gardens still to be found across the Islamic world. Each one serves as a vehicle to strengthen our ties to the Heavenly gardens, the gardens to which, by the grace of God, we will eventually return. In fact, historically, the four-fold garden existed in ancient Persia long before Islam: here, for practical irrigation purposes, a regular grid system of water-channels or 'rills' based on the number four was employed. As will be further discussed below, the number four itself is the geometric symbol of Earth just as the circle is the symbol of Heaven. Islam inherited an ancient, universal form and invested it with a whole new spiritual vision. Thus these earthly four-fold gardens are both a symbol and a sanctuary where peace is found and hope is regenerated: 'Exiled on earth as we are, unless we are able to content ourselves with that shadow of Paradise that is Virgin Nature, we must create for ourselves surroundings which, by their truth and their beauty recall our heavenly origin and thereby also awaken our hope.'[9]

One of the principal functions, therefore, of these earthly 'Gardens of Paradise' is to provide a beautiful and harmonious retreat from the world, where the soul can let go of distracting thoughts and attain some level of peace. The word *Islām* is derived from the root *s-l-m*, which primarily means 'peace' but also means 'submission' or 'surrender'. Therefore, together, one could understand the word to mean 'the peace that comes when

7. The word *jihād* itself simply means 'struggle' or 'effort'.

8. This is a Persian term, from Farsi *chahār* 'four' and *bāgh* 'garden'.

9. Frithjof Schuon, *Esoterism as Principle and Way* (Bedfont, Middlesex, 1981), p. 196.

one's life is surrendered to God'. The traditional greeting used across the world by all Muslims — of whatever race, nationality, colour, age or background, and regardless of whether any other words can be communicated — is *Asalāmu ͨalāykum*, 'Peace be upon you'.

The apparently endlessly flowing water in the courtyard gardens of Damascus, Fez, Marrakesh, the Topkapi Palace in Istanbul, the mosques of Isphahan, and most especially in the courtyards and gardens of the Alhambra and Generalife (at which we will look more closely later) are some of the most evocative representations of the Islamic Gardens of Paradise anywhere in the world. The sound of water not only muffles the voices of other people but has the miraculous effect of silencing one's own thoughts and giving us a taste of the peace of Paradise — the Peace which St Paul referred to as 'the peace which passeth all understanding'.[10]

To return to the Qur'ānic descriptions of the Gardens of Paradise (*jannāt al-firdaws*), we may consider some brief extracts to give some indication of the sense of rich abundance and blissful delight that a fuller reading gives so powerfully: 'therein they shall recline upon couches . . . Immortal youths shall go about them, when thou seest them, thou supposest them scattered pearls, when thou seest them then, thou seest bliss and a great kingdom' (LXXVI: 18-20); in Paradise, 'We shall strip away all rancour that is in their breasts; as brothers they shall be upon couches set face to face' (XV:46-7); there is a perfect temperate climate, 'they shall see neither sun nor bitter cold'. (LXXVI:13) There will be cool pavilions, couches, cushions and carpets and silk attire, 'green garments of silk and brocade' (LXXVI:21).[11] Weariness is unknown in this Paradise, 'there shall be repose and ease . . . no fatigue there shall smite them' (XV:46). Fruit will be in abundance, 'produce is eternal . . . such fruits as they shall choose and such flesh of fowl as they desire' (LVI:20–21) will be provided. Gold and silver jewellery will be worn, and 'sweet potions' will be drunk from 'vessels of silver' and 'goblets of crystal' (LXXVI:15): these are of such purity that there are no after-effects, 'no brows throbbing, no intoxication'(LVI:19). An essential element of the Gardens of Paradise is that they are eternal, that it is granted to the righteous 'therein to dwell for ever; that is indeed the mighty triumph'(LVII:12).

It is very moving to read that our Lord rewards the faithful for remembering Him: 'And their Lord shall give them to drink a pure draught. "Behold this is recompense for you, and your striving is thanked"' (LVII:12).

The marvellous descriptions of the *jannāt al-firdaws* transport the reader to the Heavenly realms, to a place of infinite and surpassing peace and felicity that only the most dedicated

10. Philippians 4:7.
11. Muslim men are not supposed to wear silk or gold in this life — these are reserved for the Hereafter.

spiritual seekers can reach on earth — through the constant and sincere remembrance of God (*dhikr Allāh*), through the nurturing of the garden within, the garden of the Heart. As the great poet and mystic, Jalāl ud-dīn Rūmi, wrote, 'The Real gardens and flowers are within, they are in man's heart, not outside.'[12]

The longest reference to the Gardens of Paradise in the Qurʿān is in Sūrat ar-Rahman (Sura LV: 'The All-Merciful') in which are described two pairs of gardens, four altogether — the archetype on which the four gardens of the *chahār-bāgh* are based. There is a profound and complex symbolism attached to these two pairs of gardens on which we can only touch briefly here. According to certain commentaries,[13] these two pairs of gardens reflect the dual nature of man, both human and divine: one garden for the lower or 'horizontal' aspect of man and his individual desires, and the other garden for the higher or 'vertical' aspect, concerned with the Transcendent. The two lower gardens represent the Garden of the Soul and the Garden of the Heart (reserved for the Righteous) and the two higher represent the Garden of the Spirit and the Garden of the Essence (reserved for those who are most favoured by God).[14] Just as Dante describes the hierarchy in his *Paradiso*, so there is a hierarchy in the Islamic Afterlife, and this is reflected in the different levels of the two pairs of gardens. According to the station that your soul has reached in life, you will be rewarded with the appropriate pair of gardens.

Each of the four gardens contains its own tree bearing fruit — respectively, the olive, the date, the fig and the pomegranate. The olive tree grows in one of the lower gardens, the Garden of the Soul, and in the Garden of the Heart grows the fig. In the higher pair of gardens, the Garden of the Spirit has the date-palm growing in it and in the Garden of the Essence the pomegranate is to be found. The fruits of these trees, according to the esoteric interpretation, represent the levels of purity that individual souls have attained as they are re-absorbed into their Heavenly archetype. In each of the two pairs of gardens, the lower garden contains a fruit which still has its stone (that is, the olive and the date): this stone corresponds to the kernel of individuality that still remains in the soul. In the higher garden of each pair, the fruits are the fig and pomegranate: in both cases pure fruit, all of which can be eaten. The pips, representing the kernels of individuality, have been absorbed into the One Whole.

As well as fruit, each of the four Gardens of Paradise contains its own fountain. The first pair have 'two fountains of running water' (LV:50), and the second pair have 'two fountains of gushing water' (LV:66), implying proximity to the Source. In the highest garden the

12. Quoted by Annemarie Schimmel in her essay 'The Celestial Garden', in *The Islamic Garden*, edited by E. B. Macdougall and R. Ettinghausen (Dumbarton Oaks, Trustees for Harvard University, Washington DC, 1976), pp. 11–39, at p. 23.

13. The account which follows is primarily based on Abu Bakr Siraj ad-Din's *The Book of Certainty: The Sufi Doctrine of Faith, Wisdom and Gnosis* (London, 1952; reprinted Cambridge, 1992).

14. These latter persons are called *as-sābiqūn* in Arabic: a term rendered as 'the Outstrippers' by Arberry, and as 'the Foremost' by Yusuf Ali.

15. Act V, Scene 1.

16. 'Oud or 'ud ('eagle-wood' or 'aloe-wood' in English) is understandably the most sought-after incense in the Arab world–once experienced, no other incense comes close to its beautiful and intense fragrance. It comes from the precious wood of the aloes tree, *Aquilaria agallocha* or *A. muscaria* (not to be confused with the medicinal shrub 'bitter aloes', *Aloe vera*, used together with myrrh by Nicodemus to anoint Christ's body after he was taken down from the Cross). In fact, it is not the normal wood of this ever-green tree which smells so delicious but the resin that the tree produces when infected by a fungal disease. Trees can be infected artificially in order to produce more of the resin. The 'ud tree grows in many parts of Asia: the best incense, according to the experts, is derived from trees grown in Cambodia and Vietnam.

17. Genesis 2:10. The rivers of water, milk, honey and wine can be closely paralleled in Judaeo-Christian apocryphal tradition: examples in Louis Ginzberg, *Legends of the Jews*, trans. H. Szold, 7 vols (Philadelphia, 1909–38), v.29 n. 76; M. R. James, *The Apocryphal New Testament* (Oxford, 1924), p. 538.

fountain is named Tasnim (meaning 'Exaltation' or the 'Exalted') and the supreme river is named Kawthar (meaning 'Abundance'), from which only 'those who are nearest to God' (LVI:10-11, translation by Yusuf Ali) can drink. Both of these fountains are flavoured with musk. It is no accident that Arabian countries are known for their sweet-smelling scents and beautiful perfumes (Shakespeare refers to them in Macbeth)[15] since these had the capacity — and still do if you have ever smelled the finest 'ud[16] — to arouse a remembrance of the Heavenly Gardens. The fountain in the centre of the Islamic garden represents the ever-flowing waters of the Spirit, constantly refreshing the soul. There is an inscription in the Hall of Ambassadors at the Alhambra which reads: 'The fountain in my midst is like the soul of a believer, immersed in the remembrance of God.'

I hope to have made clear from this brief summing-up of the esoteric meaning of the Qur'ānic descriptions of the two pairs of paradisal Gardens is that the four-fold form of the Islamic garden on earth, the *chahār-bāgh*, with its water, fountain(s) and trees, is not simply an aesthetically pleasing design, or a solution to irrigation: it is both these things of course but more profoundly, it is a symbol of the archetypal Heavenly Gardens and as such offers a more meaningful refuge or sanctuary from the world than does a garden without such conscious symbolism. As with all sacred and traditional art, form and symbol are one.

Let us return now to the more practical aspect — the representation of these gardens on earth, and how they can provide a sanctuary for us in more ways than the original definition discussed at the beginning of the paper. Although there are other forms of Islamic gardens, such as the larger, open and outward-looking gardens (for example, the Menara gardens and the Agdal gardens on the edge of Marrakesh), we are concentrating here on the *chahār-bāgh*. Because of its division by water-channels or pathways into four quarters (themselves sometimes subdivided), with a fountain or pool at the centre, it is the simplest, purest and truest manifestation of the Islamic Gardens of Paradise. This four-fold design was inherited from an ancient Persian prototype which embodied a timeless and universal symbolism, a symbolism which was re-confirmed and given a new lease of life by the sacred image of the four Gardens of Paradise (*jannāt al-firdaws*) in Sūrat ar-Rahmān. There is also a *hadīth* (saying) of the Prophet Muhammed in which he describes his Ascent to heaven (*mi'rāj*) and speaks of four rivers, one of water, one of milk, one of honey and one of wine. These four rivers are also mentioned in the Qur'ān (LXLVII:15), and in the Book of Genesis it is written, 'And a river went out of Eden to water the garden and from thence it was parted into four heads.'[17]

This four-fold design was eventually taken up and developed across the Islamic world. The universal symbolism inherent within the number four is based on an understanding of the natural world: it encompasses the four cardinal directions, the four elements and the four seasons — and the cube, the three-dimensional form of the number four, represents solidity, the Earth. The word Kaʿbah actually means 'cube', and it is said that the city of Mecca was originally divided into four parts by having lines drawn from the four corners of the Kaʿbah. When one makes the ʿumrah (minor pilgrimage) or ḥajj, one of the principal rites is the circumambulation of the Kaʿbah. Heaven and earth thus meet symbolically, represented by the circle and the square — and man is the link between the two. In Islamic gardens, one often finds a circular fountain set within a square base.

There is no doubt that one of the finest earthly manifestations of the Islamic Gardens of Paradise is at the Alhambra in Granada, Spain, although ironically Granada has not been under Islamic rule for centuries. Happily, the re-conquering Christians realized that in towns such as Granada, Cordoba and Seville it was as well to retain much of what their Islamic predecessors had built. It is sad to say that in many parts of the Islamic world, such as India and Iran, the gardens need much restoration — in particular the water has been allowed to dry up, depriving them of their life and soul. In Granada, the Nasrid dynasty (which ruled from AD 1237 until 1492) created a series of exquisite courtyards, in the centre of which water is always present in some form or other. Indeed, the water system that the Nasrids introduced to the Alhambra Palace and the Generalife gardens is a truly remarkable feat of engineering. Although the Alhambra is not a sacred building, in a traditional Islamic society there is no distinction between the sacred and the profane. This means that even if a building is not specifically for a religious purpose — as is a mosque — it still partakes of the fundamentally spiritual outlook of the society. Therefore the Alhambra palace is at once a seat of power and a manifestation of a society profoundly penetrated by a spiritual understanding of the cosmos. This borne out by the phrase repeated over and over again on the palace walls: Wa lā ghāliba illa-Llāh, 'There is no victor but God.' This calligraphy, and the intricate geometric and biomorphic patterns that also adorn the courtyard walls, are constant reminders of the unity of God, that He encompasses every aspect of life.

Of course, enormous changes have taken place since the Alhambra and Generalife were constructed, particularly in the planting, but in spite of that the palace courtyards and certain parts of the gardens retain a very special, quintessentially Islamic, ambience.

Previous page: Patio de la Acequia, Generalife Gardens, Granada

Although vast numbers of people are shunted through daily (at least six thousand tourists per day), if you take time to sit quietly it is possible to ignore the hordes. Occasionally the numbers diminish, and one becomes acutely aware of the sanctuary-like atmosphere of the courtyards and gardens. The first court one experiences is the Court of the Golden Room (Cuarto Dorado) entered from the Mexuar (the Conference Room), which acted as a kind of waiting-room for petitioners to the Sultan. This courtyard, like the others, is separated from the world outside and is open only to the sky and the heavens above — representing man's aspiration towards God. The privacy of the courtyard, opening inwards towards the heart rather than outwards towards the world, corresponds to the separation of the private and public domains in traditional Islamic society. It represents the inward (bāṭin), contemplative aspect of man. The courtyard is itself a kind of miniature garden of paradise, the essential ingredient being, not trees, plants and flowers, but water. However small these courtyards may be, there is always some form of running water.

From the courtyard of the Golden Room we go through a dark passageway, and out into the bright sunlight of the largest courtyard: the Court of the Myrtles (or the Alberca court, from the Arabic al-bīrka meaning pool). Here the myrtle hedges, probably planted in the late nineteenth or early twentieth century, border the large still central pool. This courtyard, together with the Hall of the Ambassadors, Sultan Yusuf's throne room on the north side, formed the main reception areas in which the Sultan could entertain ambassadors and foreign rulers. It is a most harmonious and beautiful balance between architecture, water and vegetation.

From this court we proceed through another dark passage (a typical element of Islamic architecture, which gives a sense of anticipation and mystery, as well as increasing the sense of privacy): this time to the famous Court of Lions, built by Muhammad V in the late fourteenth century. This is a classic chahār-bāgh design, probably originally a private area for use mainly by the Sultan and his family. It must be remembered that the four quarters of this courtyard were originally luxuriously planted with shrubs, flowers and herbs rather than the rather meagre-looking four citrus shrubs, one in each quarter, to be seen today. With increased planting the court would be a more harmonious balance of architecture, water and vegetation: beautiful as it is, the glare of the sunshine would be softened by the cool green of foliage. Titus Burckhardt describes the Court of Lions as follows:

The plan of the heavenly garden always includes the four rivers of Paradise flowing towards the four quarters of heaven, or from them towards the centre. The water-courses of the Court of Lions are fed from the two halls to the north and south and from the two stone canopies at the west and east end. The floor of the halls is set higher than the garden, and so the water, which flows from round basins, runs down over the threshold towards the fountain, where it collects around the lions and soaks away . . . . The fountain itself with its twelve lions supporting a basin spewing water is an ancient symbol which reached the Alhambra from the pre-Christian Orient by way of all kinds of intermediary links. For the water-spewing lion is none other than the sun, from which life gushes forth, and the twelve lions are the twelve suns of the Zodiac, the twelve months that are all present concurrently in eternity. They support a 'sea' . . . and this sea is the reservoir of heavenly waters . . . . The stone canopies, too, at opposite ends in the east and west of the garden, are also a part of the picture of the garden of paradise, for in the description of paradise, the Qurʾān mentions high canopies (*rafraf*) or tents.[18]

In the gardens that extend mainly to the east of the palace (toward the Generalife), we come first of all to the Partal, the oldest of the series of palaces, built by Muhammad III in the early fourteenth century. This is a kind of pavilion with an upper floor giving views over the Sierra Nevada to the north and the gardens to the south and east. Beyond this lies a series of garden courtyards, formed not by stone walls but by hedges or trees which become nature's 'walls' and create secluded and semi-private areas. Everywhere there is water, either still — as in the large pool in front of the Partal — or flowing along channels, up through fountains and down narrow rills.

Nowhere is water more in evidence and more soothing — to the eye, to the ear and, above all, to the soul — than in the gardens of the Generalife. The name 'Generalife' probably derives from *jannāt al-ʿarīf* meaning both 'Garden of the Architect' and 'Garden of the Gnostic' or the 'One who Knows'. The Generalife palace and gardens were built originally as a country retreat for the Sultans of Granada, somewhere close by for them to retire from worldly affairs; they probably date from a little earlier than the palaces of the Alhambra, although the gardens themselves have undergone much change since the thirteenth century. The gardens cover a large area on a hillside known as the Hill of the Sun, and consist of a series of intimate spaces with tall dark cypress trees, hedges, flower-beds and — the most

18. Titus Burckhardt, *Moorish Culture in Spain*, (Munich, 1970); English translation by Alisa Jaffa (London, 1972), pp. 209–10.

important element — water. Water is everywhere, from the most simply designed fountain to the more elaborate. Originally, these gardens provided the inhabitants of the Alhambra with vegetables, fruit and even pasture for livestock. Today, most of the planting dates from the twentieth century. Some of it one might wish to alter, particularly the modern hybrid roses; nevertheless, the design, the lay-out, the cobbles and the many variations of water and fountain, all contribute to the very special sanctuary-like atmosphere which, despite the thousands of visitors, is still retained. This is a great testimony to those who first laid it out.

It was Muhammad ibn Ahmar, the first of the Nasrid Sultans, who established the Alhambra water system; he ordered a royal canal to be built which diverted the River Darro (the water of which came from the melting snow of the Sierra Nevada mountains as well as rain) along the hills towards the Generalife. The water then travelled through a series of aqueducts (*acequias*), pools, cisterns, waterwheels and reservoirs (*albercones*) to the palace-complex — and small city as it then was — of the Alhambra. This water supply is the key to the development of this earthly paradise and is testimony, not only to the ingenuity of the Arab engineers, but also to the veneration and awe that they held for water: to them it was sacred, a gift from God. To give some idea of the complex nature of irrigation in southern Spain, it is fascinating to read an extract from a book written a few years ago by an Englishman who bought a farm in the Alpujarras (next to Andalucia). He very quickly found out the importance of understanding how the water worked:

There are literally hundreds of miles of *acequias* (aqueducts) in the Alpujarras, and the paths along their banks, lined with grasses and a rich variety of alpine flowers — gentians, campanula, digitalis, saxifrage — make wonderful walking with heart-stopping views . . . . High in the mountains, way above the villages, the channels are wide streams of clear rushing water, ice-cold and lying far above any possible source of contamination, delicious to drink . . . . Hundreds of small farmers depend on these *acequias* and so an organized social system has grown up to ensure an equitable supply. Each *acequia* has its president, elected each year, each a treasurer, and its *acequero* . . . . If your land has water rights from a certain *acequia*, you are allotted a certain time and a certain quantity of water. You may be unlucky (or out of favour with the water president) and come up with, say, seventeen minutes of one-third of the *acequia* at ten past three on Thursday mornings. Accordingly you plod out to your orange grove and your vegetables with your torch stuck in your mouth and your mattock over your shoulder.

At ten past three—not nine minutes or eleven minutes past—you pull the hatch and let the great body of water tumble through on to your land.[19]

The jewel at the heart of the Generalife is the Patio de la Acequia, meaning literally 'Patio of the Aqueduct'. This garden is high up on the side of the hill; it is approached through a small courtyard, known as the Dismounting Yard, up some steps and then up more steps, dark and covered. And then, altogether unexpectedly, a small arch opens out on to what can only be described as a 'vision of Paradise'. Here we experience a taste of what the Qur'ān promises to the God-fearing: *Jannāt tajrī min taḥtiha al-anhār*, 'Gardens underneath which rivers flow'.[20] To sit in this garden for any length of time, slowly absorbing the beauty contained there, allows the sound of the water to gradually drown out all preoccupations of the soul. An overwhelming sense of peace descends, and the visitor is drawn into a state of contemplation of Divine Unity.

CONCLUSION

There seems little doubt that the *chahār-bāgh* type of Islamic garden is a kind of sanctuary: not only is it a place of refuge and contemplation but also, in its role as the earthly symbol of the Paradisal Abode, it serves as a reminder to the visitor of both the immanence and the transcendence of God. The garden may not be an area specifically set aside for prayer; but because it is such a profound symbol it serves as a powerful support in the contemplation of Heavenly realities, as well as offering a foretaste of the inexpressible peace and joy to come. As a symbol the Islamic garden can also be a reminder of who we are, especially in these difficult times: not just for Muslims but for people of all faiths. A garden which leads us back to the Heavenly Garden is a reminder that beauty is a path to inner serenity; it is an expression of faith and love, a bridge between the visible and invisible worlds. 'Look for the garden within yourself, in your indestructible Divine substance, which will then give you a new and imperishable garden.'[21]

ADDENDUM

There is a powerful parable in the Qur'ān in Sūrat Al-Kāhf (The Cave) about a vain and proud man who ignores the 'signs' of God and is convinced that the beauty of his garden

19. Chris Stewart, *Driving Over Lemons* (London, 1999) pp. 112–13.

20. This is the phrase most often repeated in the Qur'ān to describe the Gardens of Paradise: thus Sura XXII, verse 18.

21. Frithjof Schuon, *The Transfiguration of Man* (Bloomington, Indiana, 1995), p. 103.

is all his own doing and that it will last for ever, claiming, 'I do not think that this will ever perish; I do not think that the hour is coming; and if I am indeed returned to my Lord, I shall surely find a better resort than this' (XVIII:32-42). His companion is horrified at this arrogance and asks why he is not praising the Almighty for his beautiful and fertile garden: 'Why, when thou wentest into thy garden, didst thou not say, "As God will; there is no power except God"?' The companion, being a faithful and righteous man, can look forward to the Heavenly Gardens, saying to the arrogant one, 'Yet it may be that my Lord will give me better than thy garden and loose on it a thunderbolt out of Heaven, so that in the morning it will be a slope of dust.' Sure enough, because the arrogant one failed to acknowledge that he owed his good fortune to the generosity of his Lord, he was punished with a thunderbolt from Heaven and his garden became as dust.

Sanctuaries: The Journey of Immanence and Transcendence

KAPILA VATSYAYAN

The Indian landscape — forest, fields, villages, roadsides and even mega-cities — is interspersed with the sudden but sure appearance of a single stone or cluster of stones, a tree, a water body small or large, inverted clay pots hung on the branches of trees, or ash-besmeared mendicants sitting under trees or in open spaces. All these become sanctuaries, or shrines, charged with a sense of the 'sacred'. These match the temples, small or large, in built form, which invite the devotee to worship the deity in the centre of the temple. Is there a connection between these two? Or do they represent divergent and irreconcilable attitudes to the 'sacred' and the notion of sanctuary?

To this last question, the answer is unambiguously in the negative. Physical place or space becomes 'holy' — sacred — in time, and not only by virtue of being a fixed place or space. When the 'stone' is no longer consecrated with ritual vermilion and incantation (and much else), when the tree loses its power, and when the temple is in disuse, then all these are mundane or profane, and no longer sacred. It is human consciousness, with its aspiration to identify a symbol for worship, surrender or the quest for self-realization, that makes a place and space 'holy' or sacred. The great *stupas* and the many temples which are no longer ritually sanctified are not places of pilgrimage: they are archaeological monuments of great historical significance, and destinations for tourists. India provides

Facing page: Looking into the sanctuary of the Jain temple, Ranakpur

abundant examples of humble shrines, as also of monumental architectural structures, which have served for millennia as 'sanctuaries', both as sacred places and also as centres of massive congregations and places of pilgrimage.

Concurrently, there are places and institutions of seclusion, of withdrawal from ordinary life — especially from the life of 'domesticity' — which are called by the generic term *ashrama*, corresponding to the *viharas* of the Buddhists. These can be, and are, situated on mountaintops or hillsides, in forests or deserts, on river banks or sea shores. They too punctuate the Indian landscape and are not mere relics of the past. The spectrum is wide-ranging, from sanctuaries intended only for specific, monastic or sectarian orders, to those for the laity. They invite into their fold individuals of all ages and genders. Some focus on specific disciplines, or subscribe to particular faiths; others are only places for solitary contemplation and meditation, with minimal facilities provided. They can be termed forms of 'refuge', but are not places for mere escape from ordinary life. Their first essential demand is the pursuit of knowledge or wisdom through austere discipline.

The word *ashrama* also denotes a stage in human life. The Hindu tradition envisages four goals of life, known as the *purusharthas*, viz., *kama, artha, dharma* and *moksha*, roughly translated as the pursuit of desire, of wealth or economic well-being, of righteous conduct or duty, and of liberation. These four goals are juxtaposed with the four stages spanning the life of the ordinary human: from childhood and adolescence (*brahmacharya*) to the domesticity of a householder (*grahastha*), to the stage of the forest dweller or wanderer (*vanaprastha*), to that of the renouncer (*sanyasi*). There is no one-to-one equivalence between specific goals and the stages of life, but there is coherence in the system. In both cases there is a suggestion that an individual could move from the fulsome celebration of life to a gradual disengagement, i.e. withdrawal to the inner life of meditation for seeking detachment and liberation. Detachment at the moment of engagement is the highest aspiration — it is the ultimate demand made for human conduct.

The *ashrama* (i.e. stage) of the *vanaprastha*, the forest dweller, is reached after the full ripeness of the experience of life, not by its denial in self-inflicted mortification. Undoubtedly there are a few who aspire to the life of renunciation without going through the sequence of the preceding stages. They are the sages and the *rishis* of the past and present in India. They are neither saints nor monks in the ordinary sense: they are those who have experienced liberation here and now — *moksha, jivanmukti* — and need not wait to achieve it in a life hereafter. Their being and presence radiates the experience of the 'inner self' which has merged with the universal self. We learn of such figures in the past, and they have walked the earth of India in the present—be it a Ramana Maharshi or Rama-krishna or Sri Aurobindo. It is human persons, therefore, who are sacred—and sanctu-ary—and not the institutions (or *ashramas*) which may have grown up around them.

Even this brief enumeration will perhaps make it evident that 'sanctuary' in this land of diversity and plurality is a concept which has taken many forms. It is manifested in multiple ways on multiple levels; and yet the one unifying thread is the insistence on the process of gradual movement from the gross to the subtle, from the physical to the meta-physical, from the personal individual self to the seeking of a state of 'transcendence' through experience and not cerebral intellection. In what follows, I shall attempt to give a few select examples of these varied manifestations of the notion of the 'sacred' and sanctuary in place and space, as also in consecrated time.

In the groups of people whom, with an inappropriate use of anthropological termino-logy, we choose to call 'tribal', the consciousness of the sacred manifests itself in many forms. In essence, it is the explicit affirmation of the relationship of Man in Nature and not Man and Nature. All inanimate and animate being is imbued with power and spirit. Thus a stone or tree, plant or body of water, is identified as 'sacred'. The inanimate can become animate, and the animate inanimate. Transformations and transubstantiations can take place at consecrated moments. Thus a stone, a megalith, or tree becomes sacred at given moments. Ritual and celebrations are the outer manifestations.

On these specific occasions, at the level of conscious belief, the individual/community is in dialogue with the cosmic phenomena of earth and sky, life and death. The cos-mogony and cosmology of particular groups explicitly articulate this world view. The sense of the sacred is intrinsically interwoven into the fabric of life. Here, function—that is, conservation of the natural environment, maintenance of ecological balances—and cosmology and 'sacredness' and the designating of sanctuaries are all fused together. Specific trees, such as *ficus religiosa*, are considered 'sacred'. Some plants are also considered 'sacred', e.g. *tulsi* (basil). Examples are found in all parts of India, and are still extant amongst the forest dwellers such as the Santhals, the Marias and the Saoras. Anthropology has called them and their rites 'animistic', but these peoples are better seen as providing self-evident examples of the consecration and making sacred of space and time. Indeed, the humble dwellings constructed with bamboo or wood are concurrently the abode of men, gods and deceased ancestors. The world of men corresponds to earth, that of the gods to heaven, and that of the deceased ancestors to the nether world. None of these worlds is insulated, each is in dialogue with the others. The outer manifestations of this 'consciousness' are the visual symbolic forms on the walls — inner and outer — of these dwellings. For example, the Saoras of Orissa mudplaster their walls. On this surface is drawn a square or rectangular enclosure. This enclosure, drawn with a twig dipped in rice powder, becomes a sacred enclosure. It is known as 'the house of the gods'. Inside the enclosure the whole universe is visually re-created — comprising vegetation, animals, men and gods. Incantation invokes the deities to come and reside in this consecrated space and, by extension, in the whole dwelling. The invocation of the Saoras is profoundly significant. Roughly translated, it runs:

> I have made a house for you. Here are your elephants and horses. Come riding on them. Come and see what a fine house I have made for you. Deities of the sky, come and see the house. Deities of the hills, come and see, deities of the water, come and see.[1]

The painted enclosure on the wall is thus a shrine and sanctuary, which is enlivened on specific occasions with ritual ceremonies. Thus both time and space are consecrated; and yet the dwelling is the functional dwelling of the family. The division of sacred and profane is not absolute. Indeed, it is if anything temporal. Ritual brings the sacred and the divine periodically to life; but the consecrated drawing is also a reminder of these realities at all times. There are countless examples of this kind from all parts of India — Gujarat, Rajasthan, Uttaranchal, Orissa, Andhra and Kerala.

At another level, especially in the agricultural societies, the sense of the sacred and consequently of sanctuary is identified with the concept of the 'seed', or *bija*. *Bija* is a fundamental term in Indian life and thought, figuring in the terminology of disciplines ranging from agriculture to cosmology to medicine to mathematics, as well as in aesthetic theories, architectural grids, musical structures, etc. Here it is no longer merely a seed, but a major concept and technical term used to denote 'origin', organic growth process and constant renewal. Seed (*bija*) is sacred, both physically and metaphysically. It is the original latency which is embedded within the earth or the human body or the cosmic body as secret, invisible but potent power.

In the ordinary mundane or 'profane' world, the moment of embedding the seed in the earth becomes sacred. Seed is sanctified. There are special rituals and ceremonies, some

1. Quoted by Verrier Elwin, *Religion of an Indian Tribe* (Bombay, 1955), p. 404. See also Jyotindra Jain, 'Parallel Structures: Ritual Dimensions of Tribal Dwelling', pp. 120–24 in *Vistara*, published by the Festival of India, 1984.

held in the secrecy of the night exclusively by women. Later the seed is ritually placed in a pot and is consecrated in an enclosed space. Now this space becomes sacred for the duration of the ritual. There is a correspondence between sacred space and time, and neither is a frozen, fixed entity. It is the astronomical position of the sun, moon and stars, and the agricultural season for actual planting, which determine the sacredness of space and also of time. Again, there are countless examples and variations of the manner and methods of making sacred both space (or place) and time. It is this identification of seed as sacred which recalls the myth of origin. In the course of time, or even simultaneously, seed, cosmic egg and womb become cognates. Each denotes the secret power of creation and birth, and each is 'secret' because full of potency. Energy, fertility and creativity, along with organicity and the constant process of growth and change, are implicit in the notion of identifying seed as sacred in place/space and time.

While this is not the occasion for dwelling at length on the several rituals and ceremonies of embedding seed, and of celebrating the crop's final return to seed in the annual calendar, a brief description of ritual performance through a well structured choreography within consecrated space may help to communicate the sense of the sacred and of sanctuary.

One among these profoundly significant ceremonies is the ritual performance called *Nata Sankirtana* — one of the many ancient forms of ritual music and dance to which Manipur is the home. Here the embedded 'seed' of life is represented by the central pole. The ritual performance moves on many levels, dramatising cosmology as well as the myth of Krishna and Radha.

The performance is held in the open, in a specially erected *mandapa* (enclosure). A centre is established. A 'seed' is ritually embedded. At the centre a pillar, a bamboo tree trunk or banana tree, is placed. This represents the *axis mundi* uniting heaven and earth. It also signifies the *Kalpavriksha* (the Wish-fulfilling Tree);[2] and for the devotee of Vishnu, Shri Chaitanya Mahaprabhu.[3] Around this pillar is the sacred enclosure (*mandapa*). There are eight more pillars, each representing one of the eight cardinal directions. These eight pillars also symbolize the eight *sakhis* (women companions) of Krishna. Thus there are the levels of seed and tree, pole and *axis mundi*, and the Vaishnava godhead and devotees. All levels are concurrent. Though the performance is circular, the area in which it is enacted is a square, facing the east. At the south-west corner sits the *Mandap Mapu* (usually an eminent Brahmin scholar), presiding over the total performance of the *Sankirtana*. Near the

2. *Kalpavriksha* literally means 'Time Tree' or 'Tree of Time' (from kalpa 'aeon'); it approximates the symbol of the Tree of Life in other traditions, and is often called the 'Wish-fulfilling Tree' on account of its miraculous properties. In the terminology of the Bhakti ('Devotion') movement which arose in medieval India, the *Kalpavriksha* denotes centrality but also verticality: the human's journey not only revolves around the *Kalpavriksha* but is also, like the *Kalpavriksha* itself, one of gradual spiritual ascent. Many ritual performances in India establish a 'pole' or tree or banana stalk as denoting the *Kalpavriksha*.

3. Shri Chaitanya Mahaprabhu (1486-1553), a saint-poet of medieval India, was the founder of a particular branch of Vaishnavism (devotion to the deity Vishnu) which is known as Gaudiya Vaishnavism. For Chaitanya, Krishna is the Universal Soul and all human beings are his companions (*gopis*); he is Man, and all human beings are females. The relationship between them is one of lover and beloved. Devotion is the chief characteristic of Gaudiya Vaishnavism, a devotion suffused with a sense of communion and companionship as a one-to-one relationship: hence it is called *Sakhi-bhava* (female companion emotion).

middle pillar, at the western side facing east, sits the conch blower. A little further away from the performing area, at the north-west corner, is the enclosure for the *Arampham* (officiating priest), who looks after the whole ceremonial arrangement. He signifies *Bhagavati Puranamasi* — a *sakhi* who, as it were, presides over the re-enactment of the dance in the primordial space of Vraj where Krishna held his *Vraj Lila*.[4] The *mandapa* is, for the duration of the performance, a 'cosmos' on earth. Women are seated at the northern and western sides of the performance area while men occupy the southern and eastern sides.

Any *Bhakta* or devotee wishing to make an offering to the *Sankirtana* enters from the western side, where there is an opening. Offerings follow a strict routine of time and order, including the path taken inside the *Sankirtana mandapa*. After the commencement of the *Sankirtana*, no member of the audience can enter or leave the *mandapa*. For the duration of the performance it is sacred consecrated space, in 'another time' or 'no time'.

Before the *Sankirtana* starts the *Arampham* offers *dhoop, deep* and *chandan* (incense, light and sandal paste): first to the central pillar (i.e. the centre of the universe), then to the performers, and then to the gathered *Bhaktas* (devotees). White clothes are offered to the performers; this signifies formal sanctification of the artists for the day.

For all those who take part in this event, this is the offering of the mortal to the pure flame of the immortal. A *Nata Sankirtana* performance is normally of five hours' duration. It is divided into five sequentially structured sections. Normally there are sixteen male dancers, divided into two groups. Some amongst these may be as old as eighty years or more. The first is led by the main singer, called *Ishei Hanba*. The second group is led by a respondent singer, called *Duhar*. Two drummers are most important. The main drummer is called a *Pung Yeiba* and the second *Tung Hanba*. As soon as the officiating priest takes his seat, space is transformed and consecrated. The first section is known as *Adhivasa*. The second section begins with the entry of two *Pung* players (*mridanga* drum players). The president of the assembly indicates the *raga* (melody) which will be sung and this marks the ritual metamorphosis of the performers into *Sakhis* (companions of Krishna). The third section begins with the chief singer offering salutations to the Lord and the assembly. He and his assistants symbolize Gourchandra (i.e. Chaitanya). Special metrical compositions are played. The fourth section begins with the playing of a particular metrical pattern called *Rajamela*. It begins with slow measured rhythms and gradually culminates in a crescendo. This symbolizes the union of Krishna and Radha. Of special significance are the movements of the two groups clockwise and anti-clockwise: intricate choreographical

4. Vraj is the name of a place, while *lila* means divine sport or play. The 'play or sport in Vraj' refers to the dance of Krishna with the *gopis*, as this is described in such works as the *Vishnu Purana* (second to fourth century CE). Besides being an earthly location, Vraj is a divine place in the imagination and can be recreated in any place at specific times. *Vraj Lila* is enacted today in many parts of India, but especially in Vrindavan in Uttar Pradesh, and in Manipur.

patterns are formed. Questions are asked by one group, and answered by the second, only through singing and drumming and the abstract mnemonics. The leaders of the first group and the respondent singer carry on a dialogue through singing, drumming and dance, all invoking Krishna. The next section is called *Tanchup*. This is a period of rest, peace and harmony after the ecstatic union.

Manchup follows. Now is the flowering anew of life on earth. Thus the performers present, through their drumming and dance, the universe of plants, animals, birds, men and women—all living matter. It is a total participation, with complete dedication and merging of individual entities into a collective totality: differentiation is lost. The centre and periphery are in incessant dialogue, the one is many and the many one.

Space is consecrated, so is time. Finally, a mood of prayer and dedication envelops the whole assembly. There is 'silence', and gradually all leave to return cleansed and renewed to ordinary life. The enclosure is ritually dismantled and the ground again made smooth. It too returns to ordinary earth. The cosmos is ritually made and unmade. This is 'sanctuary', the holy place in time.

If the *Nata Sankirtana* of Manipur illustrates one methodology of making place/space and time sacred through recalling the secret moment of embedding the seed and its flowering through music and dance, the Vedic *yajna* (commonly translated as 'sacrifice') is the most structured ritual for consecrating space and time. The ritual undertakes the reconstitution of the universe, through the dismemberment and subsequent restoration of the cosmic Man. There is a copious scholarly literature on the Vedic *yajna*. Here an attempt will be made to describe it briefly: to make explicit the methodology by which space or any place can be ritually sanctified to become a sanctuary, and sacredness can be evoked in circumscribed time.

Vedic rituals (*yajnas*) are described in the Vedas, particularly in the *Yajurveda* and the *Shatapatha Brahmana* texts, roughly dated to 2000-1500 BCE. A piece of land is identified. It is carefully ploughed, levelled and tested for its fertility. Seeds are embedded. If they sprout, as they should, then the land is appropriate for holding a *yajna*. An enclosure is made by carefully measuring the land; the unit of measurement is now Man, or the person who is chief organizer or initiator of the ritual. Three altars are built within the enclosure, each signifying a different order of space. There is a square altar called the *ahavaniyas*, representing celestial space; the second, the *garhapatiya*, is in the shape of a circle, representing terrestrial space; and the third, in the form of a semicircle, represents the human domestic space. The metaphors of the seed and the womb are employed consistently. The circular altar is likened to the womb, and further comparisons are made between the womb and earth. The 396 bricks that are laid in layers on the square altar represent the year's 360 days plus the 36 days of the intercalary month. The five layers also signify the five elements, the five sheaths of the body and the five senses. Elaborate rituals of fire are now held in the three enclosures, simultaneously or sequentially.

Each ritual act is precise and calculated. Without elaborating on the complex rite, which is structured on the basis of meticulous mathematical and astronomical calculations each of which takes the human body as its unit of measurement, it should be sufficient to state that the Vedic ritual — especially the *agnichayana*[5] — represents the most elaborate methodology for making, for creating, sacred spaces or sanctuaries. It must also be remembered that the construction of enclosures and the building of altars to exact measure are not by themselves sufficient for sacredness. The incantations of the several groups of priests, each chanting both sequentially and concurrently, and the presence of the human couple, are indispensable for the total efficacy of the *yajnashala* (sacrificial altar). It is this total configuration that makes place and time holy, sanctified. Of equal importance is the fact that — the ritual over, having lasted for five or for twenty-one days — the enclosure, the altars and all else are ritually annihilated, burnt. Everything done on this earth, in specific time, is but a replication and recreation of the 'cosmos' and the Primordial Cosmic Man, who is dismembered and re-membered. No permanent signs remain of the great *yajnas* which were held in the past, remote or recent. The earth is renourished and fields come up and grains grow on the very ground where these cosmic events were re-enacted. The residual experience of participators is one of transformation and cleansing of the without and the within.

The parallels between the contemporary ritual performance of Manipur and the Vedic ritual can be easily discerned at the essential level. Of course, there are countless differences in structure. Vedic rituals are still performed, but they are rare and are threatened with extinction. The *Nata Sankirtan* too is certainly in danger of becoming a stage-show. However, there are the temples made of more permanent material (wood, bricks, stones), of varying sizes and shapes, of modest or monumental proportions. Viewed purely historically, it would appear that there is no direct connection between the temple and the Vedic *yajna* described above. Archaeological evidence cannot establish a direct development: there are no physical remains of Vedic ritual sacrifices.

5. The term *agnichayana* designates a special category of rituals involving fire (Sanskrit *agni*), described in the Vedas and in seminal ritual texts called the *Brahmanas*, especially one called the *Shatapatha Brahmana*. Although the frequency of such rituals is diminishing they continue to be performed, embodying an unbroken tradition of remarkable antiquity; a major *agnichayana* was held in 1975. More information may be found in Fritz Staal's massive study *Agni* (Delhi, 1984).

The earliest temples so far discovered belong to the fourth century AD. They are predated by Buddhist *stupas*, such as Bharhut, Sanchi and Amaravati. And yet, at a deep level, the conceptual plan of the temple is convincing proof that it endeavours to do in physical space what the *yajna* did in the circumscribed time of five, seven or twenty-one days. The Vedic enclosure, which was ephemeral, suggested different orders of space: the three altars were the concrete symbols of these. Through the carefully planned and executed ritual, the cosmos was made anew. Time was as if corrected, and cosmic balance restored. In the case of the temple, the structure itself becomes the replication of the 'cosmos'. We have spoken of the importance of the notions of the seed, the tree and the pole — in the context of the ancient Vedic *yajna*, as also of the contemporary ritual performance of the Nata *Sankirtan* of Manipur.

The temple is an architectonic articulation of the same fundamental conceptions. The essentials are similar if not identical. The metaphors of the seed, of the tree and final fruition, of the pole and of the image of Man, of the reciprocal relation of microcosm and macrocosm, are common despite important differences at the level of structure. Also, there is extensive variation in proportion, in style, and in the figurative and non-figurative visual narratives on the inner and outer walls of the temples of different periods and regions.

We will also recall that the Vedic *yajna* ritually dismembered and re-membered the cosmic Man. The constructed temple or *prasada* should, so the texts on architecture tell us, be worshipped as *Purusha* (Man). But what is this *Purusha* as temple which should be worshipped? The conception of the *Purusha* takes us back to the *Rig Veda*: in a seminal hymn often quoted 'He is the entire world. From him was created *Viraj*; and from *Viraj*, *Purusha*'.[6] A reciprocal process of autogenesis is suggested. Who is *Purusha*, and who is *Viraj*? *Purusha* is Man, but Man understood as a term of reference, a paradigmatic model. *Viraj* is the cosmic intelligence ordering the process of manifestation, and it is from that cosmic ordering intelligence that the first impulse of generation is spontaneously born. The two terms suggest the experiencing microcosm and the experienced macrocosm, and the reciprocal relationship of Man and the cosmos. In essence, they also refer to the process of manifestation. The world of forms is created and recreated only to suggest the experience of that which is beyond form. The temple structure too is a meticulously planned strategy through which an enormous world of forms is created, with the single purpose of evoking the experience of what is beyond form. Texts on architecture are replete with

6. *Rig Veda* X.90.

descriptions and interpretations of these concepts. The actual temple structures concretize these perceptions through brick and stone.

Before we address the question of transforming the notion of *Purusha* into the form of a building, however, let us return for a minute to the preliminary rites of choosing a site for the temple. As in the case of the Vedic ritual, 'seed' is of primary importance. The land on which the temple is to be built is carefully examined. Water is tested, ploughing is done, seeds are grown; their germination is carefully watched for three, five or seven nights. On this purified earth a centre is identified. This is a co-ordinate of the primal seed. Now begins the process of visualizing the concept of the primordial Man as *Purusha*. This is done by first drawing a basic square: this is the home of the primordial Man. A figure of Man is superimposed on the square: this is the paradigmatic model for the built structure. Two levels of meaning are clear, amongst many others: firstly, that the space/place of the temple is sacred; secondly, that the architectural plan (ground and elevation) corresponds to the image of Man, i.e. *Purusha*. The diagram of the square is subdivided into smaller squares, normally $9 \times 9 = 81$ or $8 \times 8 = 64$. A diagram of a seated human figure is drawn on the squares. The navel corresponds to the central square and the centre of the central square is the 'seed', embryo, womb. Correspondences are established between the geometrical layout and the limbs of the human form. An early text, *Agni Purana*, says that the door of the temple is the mouth of the *Purusha*, the *skanda* (the platform terminating the trunk of the superstructure) represents his shoulder, the *bhadra* or projection the arms, the wall the *jangha* (thighs and legs), and the lowermost mouldings the *paduka*, the feet. The image in the temple, the icon (*pratima*) is the very life and soul (*jiva*) of the temple.[7]

All of these descriptions serve as terms of reference, a systematized imagery, and are of course not to be taken literally. Nevertheless, this imagery provides a frame, which serves as the *skeletal* metaphor of the built form. The architectural plan is called *vastu panjara* (the architectural skeleton). The geometrical grid comprises the square which is, as mentioned above, subdivided into smaller squares. A diagram of a seated human is drawn on this square. This is called *vastu purusha mandala* (the architectural enclosure of man). The central point of the central square of the square grid conceptually corresponds to the 'seed', embedded and invisible. The central square corresponds to the sanctum and is thus appropriately called the *garbhagriha* (literally 'womb-house'). Here the icon or image is installed: this is the point where all energies converge, and from which all energies flow. The monument unfolds from this centre, both vertically and horizontally. The imagery of

7. The *Agni Purana* (literally 'Fire Purana') is one of the eighteen principal *Puranas*; Chapter LXI.11 describes the architectural grid of the temple. See further Stella Kramrisch, *The Hindu Temple*, 2 vols (Calcutta, 1946), i.55–7; and Kapila Vatsyayan, *The Square and the Circle of the Indian Arts* (New Delhi, 1997), Chapters 4 and 5.

the *Purusha* is the organizing principle of the built form. Mass is as if piled, one part upon the other, in different shapes and forms, to suggest and evoke the presence of *Purusha*.

The *prasada* (temple) as *Purusha* is meant to be seen from the outside, almost like the surface or skin of Man. The first visual impact is made by the proliferation of figurative art in low or high bas relief. Every inch of outer wall is covered, almost crowded. However, a closer look makes it clear that each moulding, each lintel, follows a careful design. Each part is interrelated with all the others. In its totality, the temple becomes at once tree, *axis mundi*, pillar, mountain and Man. The vertical grid begins from the bottom and rises to the top, culminating in the finial of the main shrine. The lower panels and lintels are filled with reliefs of aquatic and vegetative life. There are serpents and reptiles, crocodiles and others. Imperceptibly, they are transformed to lotus stalks, and the lotus stalks become creepers of mighty proportions. Slightly higher, animals appear — deer, horses, elephants, camels and many more. They are all joyous, moving in procession or seen in friendly combat. And still higher appear the female forms entwining trees. Their beautiful sensuous form, in a variety of graceful movements of the dance, has given them the appellation of 'those who embrace the tree' (*shalabhanjikas*) or 'beauties of heaven' (*surasundaris*). In no case are they enchantresses, or symbols of temptation. Then there is the panorama of life — men, women, children in their myriad moods of love, laughter, hate or disgust; but all these are as if fleeting and transient. Each figure and mood leads to the next. This is life in all its celebrations. But gradually the figurative forms decrease until they totally disappear. There are only the geometrical forms which rise to the pinnacle. And finally there is a coping stone in the shape of a seed. This is the finial, corresponding metaphorically to the head of the *Purusha*. From a distance it would appear that there is a cascade of architectural members flowing from top to bottom.

Horizontally, the pattern is repeated in different ways. The *garbhagriha* literally houses the deity in a specific iconic form. There is sometimes no icon — or only the *lingam* and *yoni*, as in many Shaivite temples. This is the most sacred space. At the threshold there may or may not be a door, but there are nearly always the figures of *Ganga* and *Yamuna*, the two river goddesses. These protect the shrine. There are a very few images on the inner walls and pillars. Often these may be only full lotuses or other roundels on the pillars supporting the enclosures. However, there is a coordination between the reliefs of the inner and outer walls. Different enclosures are created, known familiarly as *ardhamandapa*, *mahamandapa*, etc. It is not necessary to describe these details here. For us, what is important to note is the fact of creating a distinct type of holy place or sanctuary through a complex multilayered architectural schema. This is comparable to all that happens in the construction of *stupas*, churches, mosques and synagogues. Each is a specific method of evoking 'sacredness'.

In the case of the temple, the devotee's journey begins as he enters the gate. As soon as he is in the outermost enclosure he is in sacred sanctified space. He begins to circumambulate in an anti-clockwise direction. With each circumambulation, he moves gradually from the outer enclosure toward the main shrine. Then he moves in a straight line toward the *garbhagriha*. The sanctum is dark and dim, sometimes stark in its austerity. The devotee/pilgrim now reaches the threshold. He is as if face to face with the primordial energy concentrated in the image, or in the space of the womb-house. Now another reciprocal relationship is established. Through the ritual acts of offering sound (incantation, music), smell (incense), sight (through the lighted lamp), taste (through food) and touch, he is vivifying the image. By this process he is offering all sense perceptions, and the five elements of earth, air, water, fire and ether, to the icon symbolic of the cosmic being, the *Purusha*. The moment of giving, of surrender, is the moment of receiving benediction, grace, whatever. This is 'sanctified time'. The residual experience is of cleansing and renewal. The doors of the sanctum are ritually closed, or a curtain is drawn. The *Purusha* of the temple, the *jiva*, returns as if to his eternal sleep and the devotee returns again to the world of many forms. The wheel comes full circle. There is freedom from bondage and attachment, even if only momentarily. This is sanctuary, both physical and psychical. The ultimate sanctuary resides in the heart of the devotee. It is appropriately termed *hridaya akasha* (the emptiness, as also fullness of ether, within the heart).

Perhaps it will be clear even from this brief account, altogether too sketchy, that the things described—be it the *Nata Sankirtan*, or the Vedic *yajna*, or the temple and its rituals— all represent diverse methodologies for searching out and experiencing perfect equanimity between the outer and the inner, the lower self and higher self, the world of forms and the experience of that which is beyond name and form (*nama* and *rupa*). From the *Rig Veda* to the *Upanishads*, and from these to the texts called *Puranas* and to those of ritual called *Agama*, there is the constant refrain of movement from the immeasurable and the unformed to forms, multiple forms and to what is beyond form.

It will also perhaps be clear that the normal dichotomy of the sacred and the profane does not strictly apply either to the performative ritual acts of the *Sankirtana* or the Vedic ritual, or to the temple. 'Sacredness' is enacted in a specific space and time, but there are no absolute polarities.

But, as was mentioned at the start of this essay, there are also other types of sanctuaries. The third stage of life, called *vanaprastha*, is that of the wanderer, the forest dweller. Having experienced the life of the householder and domesticity, the celebration of life through both ritual and conduct, the individual is now free to seek his personal salvation along any number of paths. He is outside the confines of the social order, the community. His journey can be 'single', alone, through forests, along river banks or sea shores, or in desert caves. He returns to 'Nature' and endeavours to communicate with the perennial sources of Wisdom. At this stage, he is a 'seeker' through paths he evolves for himself. He is not yet at the fourth stage, that of a renouncer or *sanyasi*. He may choose to go on to that, or to confine himself to being a forest dweller. Sometimes an *ashrama* may become his abode, but not necessarily.

The institutions called *ashramas* are indeed sanctuaries of withdrawal, retreat and refuge. They have played an important role in maintaining balances in the social order, precisely because they lie outside the normative framework of society. The *ashramas* are vividly described in epic literature. We will recall that Sita, the heroine of the *Ramayana*, retreated to Valmiki's *ashrama*. It is in this *ashrama*, perhaps, that the epic was created. There are innumerable references to such places in Sanskrit literature, and today many of the contemporary *ashramas* trace their origin to one or another of these passages. This gives them and their lineage of teachers (*gurus*) legitimacy and prestige.

Ashramas (retreats, refuges, educational institutions around a guru or preceptor) are of many kinds. In some, particular branches of knowledge are pursued by the young and the old. Some provide place and space for individual contemplation and meditation. There are others which insist on both individual meditation and also social work—education, health, environment protection, etc. Some of these institutions have played an important role at the time of natural disasters such as drought, famine, earthquake, etc. There are also *ashramas* specifically for women who retire to these institutions before or beyond wedlock. Women preceptors have held great power, precisely because through renunciation they have expanded their consciousness to embrace a larger humanity with compassion and care. Anandmayi Ma is an outstanding example of a highly evolved human, who radiated affection and compassion and provided a healing touch. Mother Teresa belonged to a particular religion and she has left behind the great legacy of the Sisters of

Mercy. Anandmayi Ma and a few others became centres of attraction purely through their individual development — call it *sadhana* or *yoga*.

Paul Brunton describes his journeys to the sanctuaries of persons or presence in his books, especially *A Search in Secret India*.[8] There have been accounts of those who have seen and communicated with Ramakrishna, Ramana Maharshi, Sri Aurobindo and Krishna Prem, amongst others.[9] These humans, called sages, *rishis*, or evolved Beings, all turned inwards to experience that perfect state of beatitude, *samadhi*. The path, the journey, the sudden happening, was different in each case. Ramakrishna's experiences came early, as if in a flash. Ramana experienced death to wake up to another dimension of life. Aurobindo evolved from a revolutionary to a Yogi. Krishna Prem was transformed from an English pilot and teacher to a devout Vaishnava. And yet they all sought and found the sanctuary of the heart (*hridya akasha*) and peace and equanimity of the heart (*hridya vishranti*). The *ashramas* that developed around them did not come about through intellectual design. They evolved around the magnetism of their total Being. It was their person which was the 'sanctum', the place of refuge for multitudes or for a select number of individuals.

Not surprisingly, the institutions which grew in and around them have been the instrumentality of altruistic work in many fields. As in the Buddhist Sangha, their followers and affiliates are dedicated to the cause of the greater good of the wider community, or of humanity as a whole. The phrase generally used, *Loka Kalyana* ('people's welfare'), denotes the goal of doing selfless service for humanity.

Sanctuary is a journey from the ordinary mundane world of many forms, attachments, engagements and self-centredness to a concentrated effort to see the unity behind the diversity of forms, from attachment to gradual disengagement; it is a movement from self-centredness to expansion of the self, and a return to the world with a rejuvenated energy for detached action.

Perhaps three brief quotations, from Sri Aurobindo, Ramana Maharshi and Krishna Prem in Madhava Ashish's voice (Madhava Ashish was also an Englishman), will make everything which I have tried to say clear. These are the voices of the Masters.

Spirituality is not a high intellectuality, not idealism, not an ethical turn of mind or moral purity and austerity, not religiosity or an ardent and exalted emotional fervour, not even a compound of all these excellent things; a mental belief, creed or faith, an emotional aspiration, a regulation of conduct according to a religious or ethical formula

8. First published in 1934, this has just been reissued by Cosmo Publications (2004). See further Brunton's books *A Hermit in the Himalayas* (Madras, 1934) and *Inner Reality* (London, 1970).

9. The following books about these teachers, selected from an extensive literature, may be of use to the interested reader. Swami Nirvedananda, *Sri Ramakrishna and Spiritual Renaissance* (Calcutta, 1940); Paul Brunton, *A Message from Arunachala* (Bombay and Calcutta, 1969); K. R. Srinivasa Iyengar, *Sri Aurobindo* (Calcutta, 1945); Dilip Kumar Roy, *Yogi Sri Krishna Prem* (Bombay, 1975).

are not spiritual achievement and experience. These things are of considerable value to mind and life; they are of value to the spiritual evolution itself as preparatory movements disciplining, purifying or giving a suitable form to the nature; but they still belong to the mental evolution — the beginning of a spiritual realization, experience, change is not yet there. Spirituality is in its essence an awakening to the inner reality of our being, to a spirit, self, soul which is other than our mind, life and body, an inner aspiration to know, to feel, to be that, to enter into contact with the greater Reality beyond and pervading the universe which inhabits also our own being, to be in communion with It and union with It, and a turning, a conversion, a transformation of our whole being as a result of the aspiration, the contact, the union, a growth or waking into a new becoming or new being, a new self, a new nature.

Sri Aurobindo (1872-1950)[10]

The Self is the unique and only possible perfection. If realized, it will of Itself remove all the ignorance and imperfections in man, just as a lamp dispels the darkness in a room where it is burning. Here lies the secret of the so-called instantaneous and irrevocable 'conversions' and inner illuminations, well known in the past, as also in our own time . . . .

There is no such thing as chance or accident. From the point of view of the limited ego-mind such things apparently exist, but the ego-personality, based on the twofold illusion of the separate being, cannot see any sequence in cause and effect. It this is so, and it is a fact, then a true disciple on the Path need never be anxious about anything.

The much discussed and mysterious ability to abide in the Infinite Self, which transcends one's personality, is almost impossible to convey in the language of our mind-brain, which can build only mental images based on what it already knows in embryo.

Man must visit another realm — beyond the capacity of his mind-brain — if he would know the immanent Real beyond the conditioned thinking.

Ramana Maharshi (1879-1950)[11]

Freedom, then, lies only in our innate human capacity to choose between different sorts of bondage: bondage to desire and self-esteem or bondage to the light that lightens all our lives, 'Something which lies away above all, and is — It alone — truly free, solely and essentially itself' (Plotinus. VI.viii.21). To freely choose to bind ourselves in ever-increasing servitude to the Light eventually wins for us identity with the unlimited, the free.

Krishna Prem (1898-1965)[12]

10. Sri Aurobindo, *Growing Within — The Psychology of Inner Development: Selections from the Works of Sri Aurobindo and the Mother* (Pondicherry, 1992), p. 16.

11. Mouni Sadhu, *Way of Self-Realisation* (London, 1962), pp. 25–6.

12. As narrated by Madhav Ashish, *Relating to Reality* (New Delhi, 1998), p. 99.

The Making of the Sanctuary

CHARLES MORRIS and MARK HOARE

In 1998 the Prince of Wales asked Charles Morris to design and build him a Sanctuary at Highgrove. The brief for the building was simply this: it should feel like the sort of place above whose door might be written Jesus's words: 'Where two or three are gathered together in my name, there am I'.[1]

Who can precisely pinpoint the genesis of a design? The mind should not be dominated by any one preconception, but should be sufficiently free to allow a host of influences to play their part and take their appropriate place. And yet no single influence should be allowed to overshadow the one purpose of the Sanctuary: the making of a place where the spirit can soar, and where Heaven and Earth can meet.

The various influences were as follows: there was the natural wooded setting, the glade already cleared with its path leading from the garden and the narrow space between the trees through which a building might be glimpsed from the house; there was the nature of the local building materials and the desire to use them in a manner which suited their nature; there were Keith Critchlow's studies of sacred geometry, which included measuring His Royal Highness.

Charles Morris matched these outer influences against certain inner aspirations of his own: firstly that the space within should be intimate and at the same time reveal a wider

1. Matthew 18:20.

Facing page: The Sanctuary in Snow

dimension; and secondly that it should reflect the forms of the early Christian church.

There was never any doubt in his mind that this building should be designed from the inside, where the true meaning and spirit of the building should be focused, and that the form and the architectural detailing of the exterior should be an outward expression of the place within. Nevertheless, it is the exterior which must declare the building's affinity with the Earth and also its harmony with its immediate setting: this is seen in the choice and the handling of the exterior materials (of which more is said below); also in the manner in which the stone columns which support the interior vault extend through the doorway and continue outwards as free-standing columns at the entrance threshold — creating a synthesis between the trees of the Arboretum and the building itself. This is further expressed in the foliate carving of the column capitals.

It is the essence of a holy place that it should be a gateway to Heaven and for this reason the threshold and the floor of the building are sunk slightly below ground level; for it is only by acknowledging that the Earth receives us that we are in a state to look to Heaven — as St Benedict instructed his monks, it is by humility that we are uplifted.[2]

As the building took shape, there were many details and fittings to design, each of which was discussed in detail with His Royal Highness: the inscribed lintel over the entrance, the fireplace, the decorative plasterwork, the candlesticks, the chairs and settle, and most significantly of all the altar: His Royal Highness was convinced that it should be a piece of unworked natural stone with only the top worked to a level surface. There was hardly any need to explain our suggestion that the piece of stone should be cut horizontally in sections to accord with the heights of the column sections and then placed together again — a two-fold symbol of man's ability to work the stone and his respect for its natural form. This might be recognized as a theme which runs all through the building — each material is worked to a fine degree of detail, but without losing its essential nature.

The accompanying drawing shows how the limits of the space are defined by a six-foot module, which is manifest in square and cube, in circle and in sphere. The geometry is part of a Christian and Islamic tradition, consisting in the relationship of square to circle and triangle: of Earth to Heaven, with man placed between.

It was many months after the Sanctuary was designed that Charles Morris happened upon a small book by William Lethaby. Lethaby described a church built by King Alfred the Great at Athelney in Somerset: 'At Athelney King Alfred built another [church] in the shape of a cross with rounded ends — that is, quatrefoil in plan.'[3]

2. The Rule of Saint Benedict VII.1, 5–7, citing Luke 18:14.
3. W. R. Lethaby, Architecture: An Introduction to the History and Theory of the Art of Building (London, 1955), p. 142.

The similarity with the Sanctuary astounded him, and so he went to Athelney to look for the church. It was a lonely place and he might never have found anything, had he not chanced upon an elderly bearded man of whom he asked directions. The man happened to be a retired priest, who had left the Anglican Church and converted to Orthodoxy; he was also a great enthusiast for Alfred, and was able to guide Charles to the deserted place where the church had once stood. No trace of the church could be seen, except for a stone marking its place: the building had long ago disappeared into the earth.

In the Sanctuary, a sympathy with the earth is especially apparent in the choice of materials used — in the visible presence of local earth and stone in the walls, roof and floor of the building. We were intent that this sympathy should not be skin-deep, but that we should use local and natural materials throughout the building, even where they would not be seen, and we decided to avoid the use of any cement or plastic.

One of the great surprises following this decision was that the building looked beautiful at every stage of its growth. Most new buildings today fail to give much delight until the final cladding or paint has been applied — and as soon as such paint or cladding deteriorates, any delight is lost. The Sanctuary was beautiful in its making and continues to be beautiful in its life. If ever it is neglected or no longer loved, it should decay beautifully too — earth can quietly return to earth, just as Alfred's church has done.

The Sanctuary could have been built very differently and yet have looked exactly as it does — but it wouldn't have _felt_ the same. In particular, the womb-like interior has an extraordinarily rich acoustic: soft and lulling but with deep resonance too. This is as much the result of the thick earth walls and soft plasters as it is the result of the space's underlying geometry. Indeed, the earth walls are key to the Sanctuary. Keith Critchlow had suggested building with earth, and we decided to use mud-bricks (adobe/ 'clay lump') as the best practical means of achieving complex curves.

The construction process was simple but not straightforward; earth was dug from a field a few hundred metres away and tested by earth building specialist Dirk Bouwens for its load-bearing and shrinkage properties. The clay content was high, so Dirk added sand, stone aggregate and barley straw to the earth, as this helps to reduce shrinkage and cracking. He experimented with different 'recipes' and made small mud bricks which were then tested in a laboratory for their load-bearing strength. On the basis of the results from these tests, a final recipe was chosen. Dirk designed moulds for the different shaped clay-lumps to be used and had these made by a joiner. At Highgrove he then showed builders

Rodney Smith, Shaun Creed and Jeremy Hunt how to make the clay lumps — demonstrating ways of handling the heavy clay and softening it with sand, water and aggregate. Fourteen hundred lumps were needed, which were made in a lambing shed and left to dry naturally over a couple of months.

A large number of the clay lumps were stored in an area which flooded while they were trying to dry: these lumps failed to survive the deluge and the resultant mud had to be scraped up and remade into lumps. This sorry lesson illustrates a simple truth of earth construction: providing it is kept reasonably dry, earth remains strong and durable — but if it becomes 'wet-through' it is unable to hold its shape or any weight above it: this can lead to spectacular collapses! However, no earth is ever wasted — it can easily be recycled into new lumps or walls with a minimum of remixing.

Earth construction is popular in dry climates, but it is also common in Britain: clay lump, shuttered earth and cob are widespread in East Anglia, Cumbria, the Midlands and the South West. In addition, many stone buildings have structural earth at their core. When building with earth in wet places, a guiding principle is that the walls should have 'a good hat and boots': thus the Sanctuary's earth walls are founded on stone and brick footings and the roof has a generous overhang, protecting the walls from all but driving rain. Such rain isn't a serious problem, because it is rarely prolonged, and wind and sun will quickly dry out the surface of a wall.

The stone and brick footings were bedded in hydraulic lime mortar, and the base of the floor was formed in a mix of hydraulic lime and stone, laid over a chalk base. Hydraulic lime is similar to cement, in that it sets quickly, but it is more porous (i.e. breathable) than cement and, because it is manufactured at lower temperatures than cement, it causes fewer CO_2 emissions. Furthermore, during its curing lime absorbs up to 60 per cent of the CO_2 generated in its manufacture. Lime is popularly regarded as inferior to cement, but the latter is very brittle — it will snap rather than bend, and cannot easily accommodate differential ground settlement, such as might be expected in the Sanctuary's wooded environment. Rigidity shouldn't be confused with strength:

4. Sophocles, *Antigone* 712–14; cited from the translation by Robert Fagles, *Sophocles: The Three Theban Plays* (Harmondsworth, 1984), p. 96, lines 797–800.

You've seen trees by a raging winter torrent,
how many sway with the flood and salvage every twig,
but not the stubborn - they're ripped out, roots and all.
Bend or break.[4]

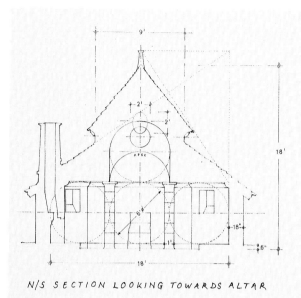

N/S SECTION LOOKING TOWARDS ALTAR

THE SANCTUARY

BUILT 1999

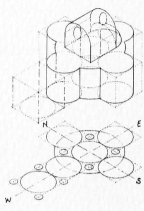

N E

W S

IN PLAN THE SANCTUARY OWES A
DEBT TO THE CHURCH BUILT BY KING
ALFRED AT ATHELNEY IN SOMERSET,
YET ITS GEOMETRY IS PART OF A WIDER
CHRISTIAN AND ISLAMIC TRADITION:
IN THE RELATIONSHIP OF SQUARE,
CIRCLE AND TRIANGLE, OF EARTH TO
HEAVEN WITH MAN PLACED BETWEEN.

THE LIMITS OF THE SPACE ARE
DEFINED BY A 6' MODULE - THIS
PRINCIPALLY MANIFEST IN SQUARE
AND CUBE, IN CIRCLE AND IN SPHERE

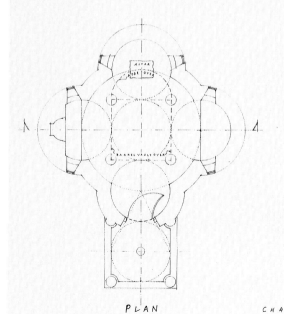

PLAN

CHARLES MORRIS F.R.I.C.S DRAWN M.W.R.H.

Drawing of the Sanctuary

The walls were built by Chris Hicks and Jason Francis, two stonemasons who had never built with earth before. The lumps were laid in an earth mortar mix similar to the mix of the lumps themselves. Each night and for many days the walls were covered with tarpaulins as temporary protection from rain, which was sadly persistent throughout the summer and autumn. Chris, Jason and foreman Nigel Selwyn bore this adverse weather with remarkable patience.

The windows are bronze-framed, set into Bath stone surrounds. The columns are also Bath stone, with 'leaf' capitals made in carver Dick Reid's workshop in York. Above the inner columns, four oak beams support a clay-lump barrel-vault. In each gable end of the barrel vault is an oval window. The reveals for these windows and the shape of the apse were formed using willow baskets made by Olivia Elton Barratt. Olivia made these beautiful baskets to great accuracy by following drawings which showed their complex shapes. Her work is now covered by plaster. The lower ceilings (also plastered) were formed with chestnut joists and split-chestnut laths. The roof structure is peg-jointed green oak, with chestnut boarding and stone slates. There is no 'roofing felt' under the slates — we have trusted the roofers to create a watertight roof.

Plastering took place in the final months of 1999: the outside of the building has an earth-lime-straw-sand plaster, whose colour is the product of entirely local ingredients. The inside has a traditional 'haired' lime-plaster. All of this work was carried out by father and daughter Steve and Johanna Welsh. Their work included a pargetted 'harvest festival' frieze on the sides of the barrel vault.

In early December Mark Hoare visited several Cotswold quarries, looking for a shapely stone which we could use as the Sanctuary's altar. We hoped that the chosen stone would be left in its natural 'rough' state except that we would cut it horizontally to provide a level top. Mark photographed and measured several candidates and presented these to the Prince — and together we chose the best of the stones, which had, it so happened, been waiting patiently in a heap in Tetbury.

The altar was set in place, its top cut level to the window cills and to the exact base of the geometric sphere formed by the apse above it — so that it is a physical and a spiritual centre in the building. Finally the floor was laid using Bath flagstones, the heavy oak door was hung, and the window sashes were fitted: four of these were glazed with clear leaded-lights, but the Prince asked John Napper to make two stained-glass windows for the East end, flanking the altar.

At the Sanctuary's inaugural blessing on 23 December 1999, low winter sun filtered through the gently swaying branches of the leafless trees around the building, projecting the windows' shimmering colours on to the bare curving walls beside them. The fire crackled and glowed and the candles danced, filling the air with the sweet smell of beeswax. The Sanctuary's life had begun.

Notes on Contributors

The Rt Rev RICHARD CHARTRES is Bishop of London, Dean of the Chapels Royal and Chairman of the Trustees of St Ethelburga's. He takes a keen interest in Russian culture and language and is chairman of the Archbishop of Canterbury's Liaison Group for the Russian Orthodox Church.

EMMA CLARK is a writer, lecturer and designer specializing in traditional Islamic art and architecture. She teaches on the Visual Islamic and Traditional Arts Programme at The Prince's School of Traditional Arts, and is a consultant in Islamic and Oriental textiles for Christie's; her book *The Art of the Islamic Garden* appeared in 2003.

GAEL ROBERTSON was born and brought up in Scotland, went on to study English Literature at Cambridge University, and subsequently trained as a photographer. She has become particularly recognized for her sensitive response to architectural spaces. *Breathing Spaces* was her first major solo exhibition; more recent commissions include the Royal Military Academy Sandhurst where she re-examined spirituality in a time of war, a project which culminated in the exhibition and publication *As Fire Fades*.

Facing page: The Westminster Synagogue, Rutland Gardens, London

MARK HOARE was the Sir Laurens van der Post scholar at The Prince of Wales's Institute of Architecture for 1995-96. He has been involved in the repair, design and construction of houses, chapels, monasteries and gardens in Britain and abroad. He won the Major Arts Award in the REEP/ACE National Schools Garden Competition in 2003, and in 2004 was one of the Lethaby Scholars of the Society for the Protection of Ancient Buildings. He now works primarily for the Soil Association.

GREVEL LINDOP is Emeritus Professor of English at the University of Manchester and Academic Director of the Temenos Academy. A poet, biographer, critic and editor, he has taught Buddhist meditation in the Samatha tradition for the past twenty years.

TALI LOEWENTHAL studied Hebrew Literature and Jewish History at University College London (UCL) and has a PhD in Hasidism. He is author of *Communicating the Infinite: The Emergence of the Habad School* (1990) and many articles. He lectures in Jewish Spirituality at UCL, is Director of the Chabad Research Unit, and is undertaking research on Hasidism and Post-modernity.

CHARLES MORRIS trained in Estate Management at Cirencester and pursued that career for six years until his interest in buildings became irresistible and in 1972 he set up his architectural practice. His work is mainly but not exclusively domestic, in all parts of the UK and occasionally abroad, hand-drafted drawings are produced for detailing every part of the building including decorative work, furniture, and its landscaping.

KAPILA VATSYAYAN is among the most eminent Indian scholars, artists and administrators. Trained as a classical dancer, she is also a linguist, diplomat, ethnographer, art historian and philosopher, who has established a range of institutions to preserve and foster the living artistic traditions of India, most notably the Indira Gandhi National Centre for the Arts. She has advised successive governments on cultural policy and has published more than twenty books, including *Classical India Dance in Literature and the Arts* (1968), *Ramayana and the Arts of Asia* (1975) and *The Square and the Circle of the Indian Arts* (1983).

The Temenos Academy is a registered charity which aims to offer education in philosophy and the arts in the light of the sacred traditions of East and West, through lecture and seminar courses, publications and audio tapes.

For further information please write to:
The Temenos Academy (Administration),
PO Box 203, Ashford, Kent TN25 5ZT.
Visit the website: www.temenosacademy.org

The Prince's Foundation promotes a return of human values to architecture, urban design and regeneration, challenging many conventional attitudes with a more integrated and innovative approach. The Foundation links ideas with practical action, drawing on a track record of teaching in the building arts, a key role in many urban regeneration and heritage projects throughout Britain and an extensive network of professionals, individual and communities.

For further information please write to:
The Prince's Foundation,
19-22 Charlotte Road, London EC2A 3SG.
Visit the website: www.princes.foundation.org

The Prince's School of Traditional Arts aims to teach Arts and Crafts skills which have profound roots in all the major faith traditions.

For further information please write to:
The Prince's School of Traditional Arts,
19-22 Charlotte Road, London EC2A 3SG.

Visit the website: www.princesschooloftraditionalarts.org